Modern Swedish Poetry

in Translation

Modern Swedish Poetry

in Translation

Edited by

Gunnar Harding and Anselm Hollo

University of Minnesota Press □ Minneapolis

Published by the University of Minnesota Press,
2037 University Avenue Southeast,
Minneapolis, Minnesota 55455
Printed in the United States of America

The following selections are copyrighted by the translators: Palm's "The Sergeant," copyright © 1972, 1974 by Siv Cedering Fox. Friberg's "The Perfectionists' Colony in Oneida, N.Y.," copyright © 1972 by Thomas and Vera Vance.

The following selections are reprinted by permission of the publishers: Transtömer's "Baltics," translated by Samuel Charters, from *Baltics*, copyright © 1975 by Oyez Press. Transtömer's "Allegro," "Citoyens," "Farther In," "The Outpost," and "Solitary Swedish Houses," from Tomas Transtömer, *Selected Poems*, translated by Robin R. Fulton, copyright © 1979 by Ardis.

Cover illustration: "Betula," by Viola Gråsten, Mölnlycke Textil AB.

This anthology was developed in cooperation with the Swedish Institute, Stockholm, and with the assistance of the Swedish Information Service, New York.

Library of Congress Cataloging in Publication Data

Main entry under title:

Modern Swedish poetry in translation.

    1. Swedish poetry — 20th century — Translations into
English. 2. English poetry — Translations from Swedish.
I. Harding, Gunnar, 1940-   II. Hollo, Anselm.
PT9590.E5R4   839.7'1'7408   78-24285
ISBN 0-8166-0870-9
ISBN 0-8166-0874-1 pbk.

Foreword

HOLDING ON TO ONE ROPE

It's a pleasure to welcome this generous and well-translated selection of Swedish poetry. This is the largest selection of contemporary Swedish work ever published in the United States. The volume doesn't include Harry Martinson or Gunnar Ekelöf, who have been published elsewhere, but it begins with their younger offspring. Because Swedish society is extremely complicated, Swedish poetry is complicated; and I'm going to provide a one-sided view of it, just to give the reader something to hold on to as he or she reads, as old farmers used to hold on to a rope in a blizzard.

I want to concentrate on one issue only, an issue that divides the poets in this book, putting some on one side, some on the other. A good place to enter the battle is with Bjorn Håkanson's attack on Tomas Tranströmer, part of which Gunnar Harding quotes in his introduction. Håkanson complains that Tranströmer's poetry has too much solitude in it — it has "images of a solitude peopled by images." Such poetry leads, Håkanson says, to a "passive, contemplative attitude toward the surrounding world: this certainly provides the reader with a fascinating experience of unimaginable distances and cosmic peace, but it does so at the expense of any impulse to intervene and to change the world."

What it means is that Tranströmer has escaped from the concentration camp of Swedish society and Håkanson wants him back in. The Swedish citizen is being ground to death, as this collection of poetry shows, between two walls. One wall is the demand for political engagement, the obligations to Africa, to the Third World, to fighting over-centralization, corruption in the government, the need to take the side of the blacks, to attack one's own male chauvinism, to stand up for those being put down, the urge to take the side of Cuba. . . . The other wall is the pressing dissatisfaction coming from inside the personality—the sense of emptiness, of the absence of love, the emptiness of the civilized psyche, whose energy gradually drains out and is not replaced, or is replaced only by self-pity, the hollowness inside, the life of reflected light, the pressure from the emptiness in the personality caused by isolation, by angers inherited from childhood, the persistent anxiety of being ignored, of not belonging anywhere, of dying without having lived.

Both these walls are made of ordinary matter, both are psychically neuter, pre-surrealist, pre-Jungian, in the sense that they are without mystery. Both walls participate actively in human slavery, as Berdyaev would phrase it. The first involves us in a slavery to the structure of society, whether as activists or wardens, as drones are slaves to the hive; the second involves us in a slavery to interior fear, that is, to the nervous ego when it becomes king and cannot be dethroned.

Håkanson's attack on Tranströmer is so interesting because he attacks Tranströmer precisely for his failure to be crushed to death between these two moving walls. Others who have escaped are Rilke, Supervielle, Machado, for each country has the walls.

I'm not saying a human being should not wrestle with the walls, but if a person's attention can be drawn away from them for a while, he or she then has a chance to enter the space of imagination, which, as Henry Corbin declares so vividly in his books, has its own laws, its own mountains, its own saints. Tranströmer describes it in his poem on Haydn:

> After a black day, I play Haydn,
> and feel a little warmth in my hands.
>
> The keys are ready. Kind hammers fall.
> The sound is spirited, green, and full of silence.
>
> The sound says that freedom exists
> and someone pays no tax to Caesar.
>
> I shove my hands in my haydnpockets
> and act like a man who is calm about it all.

> I raise my haydnflag. The signal is:
> "We do not surrender. But want peace."
>
> The music is a house of glass standing on a slope;
> rocks are flying, rocks are rolling.
>
> The rocks roll straight through the house
> but every pane of glass is still whole.

What is being described here is the imaginative world itself. This has nothing to do with passivity. I don't mean to say that Tranströmer is the only poet in this book whose work contains the "interior third world," far from it. I emphasize him because I've translated him, and his work is fresh to me. The marvelous Lapp poems of Lars Lundkvist, translated here, contain the "Haydn-world" in its uncrushed form, as do many poems of Lars Gustafsson, Gunnar Harding, and several other poets in this book. Göran Sonnevi takes the dualistic world I've mentioned, made of the Alfa Laval factory plus his own interior fears, and he treats it in an original way. He starts it spinning, at terrific speed, as if it were an atom moving in an atom smasher:

> the world's
> economy spinning faster and faster
> life and death
> going around wildly
> There's more light when I fall asleep
> I'm asleep now
> No one can wake me
> Facing the Alfa Laval factory a smaller plant:
> once the Clio Works, now
> The Scandinavian Gear Factory, Inc.
> I feel the wheels
> going faster, lights flashing on and off
> once a minute, once a second
> I'm alive in microseconds
> I'm nearly dead
> The bones in my skull
> have stopped expanding
> I'm shrinking
> I'm going around so fast
> I look motionless

A major image in Sonnevi's lively poetry, which appears again and again, is the centrifugal force that might, if we were intense enough, disintegrate the dualistic world, so that it would explode into pieces. Then it would, presumably, inherit some of the "space" it now longs for, or that the psyche longs for.

We don't have the original music of the Swedish here, since we are reading translation, so we have to read the anthology for content. I read it watching for how the poet deals with these encroaching walls. Does he or she offer the personality as a victim to the walls, as Anne Sexton and John Berryman did, or does he or she wrestle with the walls, or does he or she enter the energetic space of imagination? I read the poems that way because I need help myself in how to face the dual structure of slavery—the building Lorca leaped out of so effortlessly forty years ago . . .

Robert Bly

Table of Contents

Modern Swedish Poetry

in Translation

Introduction

It is not necessary to survey the development of Scandinavian poetry from the days of the Vinland voyages to the present: contemporary Scandinavian poetry exists within the force fields of the currents of twentieth-century poetry. The poems selected for this book were written in the last twenty-five years by fourteen poets who we think are important or typical of their time. Many other poets could have been chosen, but we thought it better to include fewer so that more poems by each writer could be presented.

Later critics have characterized Swedish poetry written in the 1950s as overly idyllic, apolitical, too private, too pallid. These are unfair generalizations. In its own way, the generation of the '50s did rebel against its predecessors, who had worked primarily in two modes: one, patriotic, idealistic, traditionalist poetry written during World War II under the threatening shadow of the Nazi invasion; the other, rhetorical, pessimistic, often anxiety-ridden modernism, ambitious in the direction of, let us say, Rilke, St. John Perse, and Eliot.

The poets of the '50s had little use for the "patriots"—in fact, by the end of the war, this kind of poetry had almost disappeared. They also rejected the pretensions of the modernists, although they were clearly influenced by them. Significantly, the poets of the '50s were the first generation that could once again travel abroad.

"Éluard flicked some switch, and the wall opened, the garden became visible," says Tomas Tranströmer. Typically, he chose the one French surrealist poet whose work has the virtues of clarity and economy of expression: Tranströmer's generation reacted against all in their precursors' work that was overblown, bathetic, too wildly and self-consciously metaphorical. They did not banish metaphor from their poems: they merely tried to make it more precise, sharper, tougher. At that time, no one admired Éluard's merits as a poet of socialism.

International artistic and literary movements obviously influenced poets like Tomas Tranströmer, Lars Forssell, and Östen Sjöstrand. Lars Lundkvist, whose poems emanate from the world of the small Lapp minority living in northern Sweden, was equally open to influences from foreign poets who combined a concern for ethnopoetics with contemporary poetic means. Although Swedish country life has been the favorite subject of most "idyllic" poetry in Sweden, Sandro Key-Åberg's treatment of it can hardly be considered provincial in any negative sense of that word. Many of the better works of the '50s have great strength and incisiveness; but one has to admit that there was also much vague, provincial, and falsely modest writing that justified later critics' strictures.

The foremost opponent of the elegiac, asocial, and introverted nature of the '50s group was poet-critic Göran Palm. In 1963 he stated: "One is looking for poems that refer to contemporary events and matters known to most human beings alive in the world today: but one finds mostly poems alluding to other poetic works, other artifacts, and matters known only to a select few. One lives in a society in which communications and contacts play a crucial part, superficial as they often are, yet quite inexorable; nevertheless, the poetry written by people living in this society often appears to close around its own secrets, seems to look away, or inward only—as if it had nothing to do with contact or communications."

Many poets responded to Palm's call for a different kind of poetry. (All of what Palm said was not really "new," since around 1930 certain Swedish poets who called themselves "Vitalists" and modeled themselves on Whitman and Sandburg had had similar ideas.) The new poetic school was called the "New Simplicity." Its members wrote about everyday settings and problems, in language almost devoid of metaphor and with little concern for musical qualities. Unfortunately, many of the poems lacked concreteness, concision, and complexity. One of the most important contributions of the New Simplists was the discovery of Sonja Åkesson, who had been writing for a number of years, totally overshadowed by her more fashionable contemporaries. Åkesson's work epitomizes the best in the productions of the New Simplicity.

In the mid-60s "concrete" poetry briefly but hectically flowered and coexisted with the New Simplicity. One of the main movers was Öyvind Fahlström, a Swedish artist who lived in New York City and sent news of the American avant-garde, its "happenings" and other open forms. Owing to insurmountable translation problems, we cannot present any examples of Swedish concrete poetry. Its prime exponent in the '60s was Bengt Emil Johnson, who avoided the artificiality and preciousness inherent in the genre by using dialect, slang, and a folksy sense of humor. Many concrete poets soon abandoned the printed book as a vehicle and worked with magnetic-tape composition. While employed by the Swedish Broadcasting Corporation's music department, Johnson made a comeback in the '70s with a number of impressive books.

Many poets of the '50s heeded the New Simplists' demands and began to write more open, extroverted poetry. Poets who did not change their style were attacked from time to time, especially as the younger generation became progressively politicized. In 1966 New Simplist critic Björn Håkanson wrote a fierce polemic against Tomas Tranströmer, the most influential poet of the preceding decade. Håkanson claimed that Tranströmer's poetry seemed to amble through the world like a well-heeled tourist: "But is it looking for us? Certainly not. It is looking for images: images of a solitude populated by images. . . . The lonely image collector's immutability is amply demonstrated by the fact that he finds exactly the same images of human beings wherever he goes, be it Africa or Sweden. . . . If one sees only what is general in the individual, and regards history as a mere agglomeration of objects and conditions, one legitimizes a passive, contemplative attitude towards the surrounding world: this certainly provides the reader with a fascinating experience of unimaginable distances and cosmic peace, but it does so at the expense of any impulse to intervene and to change the world."

By 1965 demonstrations against United States involvement in the Vietnam war were well under way in Sweden, and poets soon became active in this movement. Aesthetic questions and quarrels were shelved in favor of ethical and political considerations. Crucial texts in this debate were Frantz Fanon's *The Wretched of the Earth*, translated and published in Sweden in 1962, and Göran Palm's collection of essays *As Others See Us* (published in 1968 in the U.S.), which also deals with the colonialist view of the Third World. Göran Sonnevi's poem "On the War in Vietnam" marked the beginning of a great revival of political commitment in poetry.

Palm's settling of accounts with the '50s poets provided them and the New Simplists' successors with a language well suited to clear-cut political statement; yet the two most convincing poets of this politicized movement, Göran Sonnevi and Tobias Berggren, had other formal ideals. Although they—Sonnevi in particular— were strongly attracted to an explicit and "clear" style, both had a more extensive grounding in the complexities of linguistic and ideological theory than did poets who relied on the aesthetics of mere "simplicity." They were also far more receptive to influences from the traditions of the past. The flower of "committed" poetry in Sweden appeared in 1975: Sonnevi's large collection titled *The Impossible* was hailed as the most important book of poems to come out of Sweden in many years.

During the '60s a number of poets emerged whose concerns were far different: Lars Norén, with his dark, surrealist vision; others who in the '70s were strongly influenced by contemporary American poets, particularly Allen Ginsberg, Gary Snyder, and Charles Olson. Gösta Friberg and Gunnar Harding combine these influences, having a preoccupation with myth, legend, and Jungian psychology. As the '70s draw to a close, the slogans of the New Simplicity are attractive to only a few minor writers. There is more poetic diversity than there has been for a very long time in this small country that has such a strong tendency to box poets into "schools" and to exercise an almost superstitious belief in the numerological magic of "decades." In this climate even a rare work such as Lars Gustafsson's book of rhymed sonnets has appeared.

Comparatively and proportionately, poetry reaches a wider audience in Sweden than it does in the English-speaking world. This is reflected in the attention it receives in the mass media: the Swedish Broadcasting Corporation features poetry regularly, and all the large-circulation daily newspapers present reviews of new books of poems. Yet it is obvious that in a country of merely 8 million inhabitants the actual number of poetry readers remains quite small.

In 1967 three young poets wrote a manifesto that was sent to their fellow writers and was published in the dailies: "Most authors write for an intellectual elite, screened off from the rest of society. The channels to the general public consist of exclusive cultural journals and of the cultural pages in the daily papers which are read only by a minority and are also characterized by the individual biases of their writers. It is obvious that the presently available means of cultural distribution are highly unsatisfactory. The low sales figures also speak for themselves: on an average, a collection of poems sells some 500 copies at best, a novel, 2,000. There certainly are numerous and complex reasons for this state of affairs, but one of them is quite plain to see: our writers have done far too little themselves to try to break through the isolation they live in."

That call led to the establishment of the so-called Writers' Center. Initially, this organization consisted simply of a telephone in Gösta Friberg's study, which at that time was a kitchen in Stockholm's Old Town. This telephone became a prime channel of communication between the authors and the public. The project proved eminently successful: libraries, schools, hospitals, penitentiaries, and other institutions with government budgets for cultural activities began to invite writers to give readings and lead discussion groups. One summer a group of writers traveled by bus from town to town, stopping to give readings in public places; others were sent north in the winter to trudge through snowdrifts and recite in libraries and schoolhouses. The Writers' Center has become a large organization, affiliated with the general employment program; it employs a number of people full time and has several regional branch offices.

Before the days of the Writers' Center, poetry readings were rare in Sweden and usually were held in small literary coteries over glasses of red wine by candlelight. Thus the Writers' Center activities began a new era in the oral delivery and aural experience of poetry.

In the early 1970s Sweden's publishing houses experienced economic difficulties and this caused them to reduce their poetry lists, since these were their least profitable lines. Young poets, in particular, had great difficulty getting their works published. As a protest against the publishers' policies, they organized a large group reading in May 1973 in the Old Parliament Building in Stockholm. The reading lasted nine hours, with nearly forty poets reciting from their works; powerful amplifiers and speakers mounted on the building broadcast their words over downtown Stockholm. The audience numbered 3,000. It was an impressive demonstration, and it has since become an annual event—less a demonstration than an institution. However, the readings are no longer broadcast over the rooftops, because the loudspeakers were too successful and not only delivered poems through the walls of the Opera House and the Royal Palace but also generally "disturbed the peace."

Another consequence of the publishing crisis was that many young poets started their own "underground" presses. Mimeographed magazines with more or less fanciful names such as *Fever*, *Guru Papers*, and *Cultural Guerrilla* began to mushroom, and several poets turned to more consciously "underground" concerns and literary models. In Bob Dylan's songs and the rock music of the '60s they rediscovered both surrealism and beat poetry, and they wrote impassioned polemics with catchphrases like "Blow up the whole damned cultural elite!" and "Long live the lawless imagination!" It is a little too early to say anything conclusive about the directions their poetry may be taking. Margareta Renberg is one of this generation's less strident and most accessible poets. In any case, most of them seem lively enough to guarantee that the 1980s will not pass placidly.

Gunnar Harding   Anselm Hollo
Stockholm   Baltimore

SONJA ÅKESSON

Of the poets who during the 1960s espoused the so-called New Simplicity, Sonja Åkesson (b. 1926) would appear to be the most genuine. Many adherents to this movement were academics who theorized, in polemical and sometimes complicated articles, that poetry should draw closer to "the people" and their everyday speech and problems. Åkesson may well be the only New Simplist who truly reached a popular audience wider than the traditional one, this probably because she writes not *about* but *out of* everyday life in her country.

After six years of public school in Gotland, an island in the Baltic, Åkesson worked as a salesperson, housekeeper, office clerk, and telephone operator. Subsequently she moved to Stockholm, where, in the 1950s, she attended poetry workshops. Her second marriage was to the young 'concrete' poet Jarl Hammarberg, who on that occasion changed his name to Jarl Hammarberg-Åkesson. The couple has written and published several collaborative collections, including *Strålande dikter/nej så fan heller* (Radiant Poems/ Like Hell They Are), 1968.

Åkesson's first successful volume was *Husfrid* (Peace in the Home), 1963, which included a long pastiche of Lawrence Ferlinghetti's *Autobiography*, in which she described her life as a woman in Sweden. With an unsentimental and acerbic sense of humor she continued to deal with the loneliness and poverty of life on the fringes of a welfare society. During the 1970s a sense of desolation and pessimism became the dominant feature of her poetry. She died in May 1977.

SONJA ÅKESSON

Fatum

≪*Translated by Anselm Hollo*≫

listens to her clock
peers into her mirror

writes letters
(never acknowledged)

writes poems
(always rejected)

paints pictures
hangs them on the wall
around the mirror

"I'm not kidding myself"
she writes
"no one cares what I do
nor for me as a person
I'm not worried
but I am tired
I take too many pills"

(no reply)

writes another letter

"do you need cash?
could always lend you some
my address is
and my phone number
in case you've forgotten"

(no reply)

writes another letter

"by the way
you can have a couple of hundred
better to give away than to lend
and then be disappointed
never get it back"

(no reply)

writes another letter
encloses poems
"tell me what you think"

(no reply)

writes
"I'm not kidding myself"

scrutinizes the mirror
stares at the clock
thirty thirty-five forty fifty

To Be an Infant

≪*Translated by Anselm Hollo*≫

to be carried on the arms of daddies
as conversational bait for strange ladies

to cause obsessions
to be flung off cliffs

to be choked strangulated varnished
covered with yellow ointment
to be canned and consumed

they puke
(infants do)

they don't want to be laved in yellow ointment
they don't want to be varnished

(infants have to be varnished
all the unsightly cavities
must be varnished over)

infants must be remodeled

the festival of the infants
is known as Xmas

that's when they burble so happily
over their little porridge bowls
that's when their blue eyes shine so blue
staring at faraway chimneys

then comes the time they aren't infants
they look down on the infants
on the infants' porridge bowls

they cover themselves with yellow ointment
they stare at their varnished knees

they swaddle the infants and varnish them
they sit over their porridge bowls
spreading the stuff on the infants
working it in
into all those awful unseemly cavities

What Does Your Color Red Look Like?

≪*Translated by Anselm Hollo*≫

Heath alternating with pastureland
alternating with rocky ground.
Over here, a quarry
—where is the society for
  the preservation of nature?
Over here, a zoo
—where is the society for
  the prevention of cruelty to animals?
Over there, a village.
(A "vacation home" with pink walls)

I sit here, "thinking about love"
(and about what they call "suffering," I guess
and about what they call "sharing," I guess)

and about how stupid I am about all that

and that I do not know anything
about the "reality" you experience

nothing about the "tang" of it, the "consistency"
the "temperature"
the "images" whose marrow you suck

you, for yourself

(and what difference would it make
if I knew)

"Love"!
What a subject!

I know nothing about "love."

I could go on asking for any number of pages
about "love"
any number of pages
about the word "love"
any number of pages
about any one of all its sounds
smells, tastes
about any single one of all its meanings.

"Love"?

Yes, I have really been thinking.

There is a cold draught.
There is a fire.

There is a flush on the poor cheeks
no matter how empty and slack
and wrinkled they may be.

The thighs turn into logs
(how do you experience the concept "logs"?)
in the indifferent wind.

The lips become wounds
in the dry heat.

Heath.

Pastureland.

Mushrooms unfold
through the loose soil.

The wind grows stronger
more bitter
full of shamed memories.

There is no road
leading away.
(I put one foot in front,
the other follows)

I walk around "thinking about love"
a woman's "love," an almost old woman's:
"petrified" "disheveled" "acidulous" "insipid"
(or, on other occasions, toward other objects)
"self-sacrificing" "admirable"

my own
whose, if not mine?

I certainly "love" my cigarettes.
The more I run out of them
the greater my "love" of them.
But I also "love" the flowers
the yellow ones

(how do you experience the color yellow?)
and the bluish mauve of butterflies
hovering above them.

Not so much here when they are all around me
as in my imagination.
In my imagination
there is you, too.

In my dreams, there also are "fathomless" bogs,
church steeples swathed in black crepe
cripples, rats
(surpassing the zoo's)
"indescribable" apparitions
"hypnagogic visions," I suppose.

It happens that I find them enjoyable.
Do I "love" them?

In my dreams, there also are eyes (yours)
lips, individual hairs, wrinkles, layers of fat,
intonations, gestures (yours).

It happens that I loathe them.
Do I "love" you?

No, I don't know about "love."

I can go on asking, any number of pages
about expressions like "love" and "loving"
(and about concepts like "love" and "loving")
not getting any wiser.
I can read any number of "love poems."

"Suffering" —
that I know a little more about:
when the blotches spread on your skin
I instantly get — I suppose this is called
"hysterical tendencies"? —
blotches on mine, too.

But my fingernails remain where they are.
— No, I don't understand "suffering,"
I could go on asking, any number of pages
about "suffering"
your suffering
and be none the wiser.

What do I know about "suffering"

(I can half kill an insect
and walk away from it
unconcerned, humming a tune)

What do I know about "love" or "suffering"
I who close my eyes "voluptuously"
I who can walk about here
idle
a couple of kilometers from the zoo
the cruelty
what I understand to be cruelty to animals

I who can sing and hum
and lie and chew on grass-stalks

in this world.

I suppose we "love" one another
in our arbitrary ways?
(what tenderness for a small bumblebee
buzz buzz
among the summer flowers)

And you who "need" me.
I rush
(never getting there)
to you.

(And you who need me.
I pretend not to notice, pretend not to know,
irritably slam doors.)
Reactions.
(I am stupid about reactions)

And everything remains unanswered, as usual.

How does your heath look?
How does your color red look?
(and what use would it be if I knew?)

I would like to describe
my color red to you.
I would like to describe
(but to no avail)
my "love" to you.

What does your hunger taste like?

What did your hunger taste like, when you were a child?
(When your mother locked the door
and you heard, through it
the muffled sounds?)

"Love"?

Cruelty to animals.
(An ape sits,
"absentminded" "half-witted"
tied to a stake.
The ape breaks loose
—yes, I experienced that—
and claws a wound
onto a child's head.)

"Love"

Some kind of zoo?

A crocodile in half a liter of water?

Scores of large grey rats.

Your look that I catch
(the caged animal's look that I catch)
and hold
as long as it "suits me"?

(My hands that you bend
together, in a painful arched position
as long as it "suits you"?)

"Love"?

The funeral procession—we saw—through the village
with the two small bareheaded children
as next-of-kin mourners.
The coffin was white—
a woman, that time.

"Love"?

What a mess.

Crocodiles, rat packs, entire zoos,
cigarettes, mushrooms—decaying
before really being—
flushed old cheeks
bareheaded children.

What an "intolerable" mess.

I must help myself to clear the land
I stagger about on the heath
trying to help myself to clear it
but how impossible
how hopeless.

I'll have to go on until my dying day.

Disappointed
disappointed again
I who never "believe in anything"
—hardly even in the mushrooms'
process of decay.
(I am stupid about chemistry,
is that why I am stupid about "love"?
Is that why I am stupid about "suffering"?)

The small ants bite me, I can feel it
but I don't understand ants.
Can they get dangerous
if there are too many of them?

(I am really trying to clean it up
I keep at it, go at it, with a vengeance —
but to what avail?)

A crocodile in half a liter of water!

I am sure it is heavy, I would not be able
to lift it.

I would not be able.

The rats swarm over me
but only for hours at a time.

In between times I skip and sing.

I red, you dead.

"Bear each other's burdens"
you do it, folks.

My joints swell
dark blotches cover my skin
but my nails stay put

and in between times I skip and I sing.

The taste in my mouth is "sticky"
indescribable
(as everything else)
as the blotches on (and within) my skin,
as the specks of soil under my sturdy, faintly shimmering
fingernails.

(How do you experience my fingernails?
How do you experience the dirt under my fingernails?
How do you "evaluate" my dirt?

You whose nails are clean?
You who do not have any nails?)

Such questions.

I could go on asking any number of pages
about the "nails" and about the "dirt" and about the "love"
and be none the wiser.

I could go on asking any number of pages
about the word "dirt" and about the word "nail"

not to mention the word "sharing"
not to mention the word "love."

What is the taste in your mouth like?
All the sediments there,
in what ways does it bother you?

(and what use would it be if I knew?)

Are you trying to lift the crocodile?

(Another idea would be to pour in more water
but even there a great number of
practical problems
would no doubt present themselves)

Is it really "love" I am asking about?
Does it have anything to do with "love"?

> "Hvis det ikke var hul
>   i det ene køn
>   var kæligheden
>   fortabt
>   min søn!"

Nonsense (?)

If only the animals would not bite each other to pieces.

If only the child—the wounded one—would not scream so horribly.

It has to be endured.
Of course it has to be endured.

Other days.

Everybody has "gone their ways."
I have been left behind
(as usual) to my own devices.

I crawl about,
crawl outside:
the quarry, the zoo, the heath.

I crawl about.

    "Calm reigns in the world"
    "Love overcomes"

The confusion is (as everything else)
indescribable.

"Love"

I do not even know if I am trying to ask
questions about "love"
or about the word "love"

or if I am only possessed
by the drilling, the pounding
as of iron bars against (perhaps not granite,
perhaps not really that "hard" a rock)

by the teeming rat pack

by the taste in my mouth
and when I have become "calmer"
by my experience of the soil under the grass
by the heath with its shades of red
(and cool cool yellow).

No, it is not that I am trying to ask

but I do hold on
(I can't disengage myself)

I have to hold on

like the hungry ape, tearing
through the child's sun-fragrant hair.

"Love"
How can we talk about "love"?

Why not.

The subject of conversation is of no importance.

We can also talk about the flowers (the yellow ones)
about the butterflies, the blotches on the skin, the "suffering,"
the "understanding," the "sharing"
—we do not know what we are talking about.

The "subject" hardly matters.

Imagination "matters."
(I think of myself, full of
twistings and poundings
as if against rough-faced—well, perhaps granite, after all,
perhaps blocks of stone
that are even harder to crush.)

Then "only" the ants.

Then only the monotonous heath.

Then only shadow.
Soil.

"Love"?

Soon you come.
Soon you leave.

(And I came.
And I left.)

I speak for myself,
as the one I once was:

a young woman "who did not believe in anything"
ground to bits by "love"
("sex drive" "maternal instinct" "fear of loneliness"
  "compassion" etc. etc.)

The ants are smothering me with their "love"
but there aren't that many of them, after all.

Suddenly there are more
and what can I do?

Can you defend yourself?

The ants are a single dense black column now
and the confusion is "indescribable."

(The iron bars are bending and bending.)

Then, only a small splash in the water.

(The swelling goes down,
my joints are healing.)

So-called "reasonable proportions"?
So-called "healthy fluids"?

Other days.
We mumble "together" in the lamp's light.
You walk through the room with "special" steps.

Is it any of that?

Soon over.

I sit by the hopeless remnants
and "clean"
and "scrutinize"
and "sort out and away."

(It is obvious that I can't get it into any order.)

I could go on asking for any number of pages
about the word "love"
and about all other words
but it is the word "love" I am interested in
(and in love!)

I have thought about it a lot.

"Love"

It must have something to do with "music"?
(sometimes? Yes?)
As with the concept "lamp"
as with "water"
as with "dark"
as with "cemeteries"
as with "dog"

as with the color "red"
as with the color "pink"
as with the color "green"

(How do you experience the color pink?
How do you experience the word "pink"?)

Pink
which rhymes with love

pink
which is the skin's color
also (for me) the "inner skin's"
which (by me) is also experienced as green
—light green, speckled with jasmine
and shadow

"the color of falling in love"

"the color of cemeteries"

(How do you experience the color green?)

The big dog, guarding me
—obscuring me with his shadow—
is it "love" he feels?

Will he go wild, all of a sudden,
throw himself at me?

His hanging jowls and his sick eyes
frighten me.
(yet I am "proud" "attended"
watched over)

You chase the shadow from my cheeks.
The shadow, my shield.
(As if I had any shield)

Other days.

Shut in behind my pink walls
(what memories, hopes, sensations
of smell taste hearing
do you associate with pink walls?)
—the table, the lamp, the curtains—

nothing is yours
nor (an entirely different subject)
—and I don't mean even by way of a "loan"—
mine.

"Love"

A small boy whistles
among tiles and concrete.
I "love" him.
(I wipe his little pouty mouth
whenever I feel like it)

An old woman (my mother)
lies captive in her bed
sighing and weeping.

I "love" her.
(I listen to her moaning
whenever I feel like it)

(An old man—my father—
stumps about
in his vertiginous loneliness.

And of course I am ready to lend him my arm
whenever I feel like it.)

What do you think I mean by "vertiginous loneliness"?
What do you think I mean by "feel like it"?

No, I do not know anything about "love."

Do I "love" the words?

I use them
to no use.

Whom can I reach through words?
(and what difference would it make if I could)
Yet I use them.
Is that "love"?

All my papers destroyed by "love"!

It spreads like oil,
stifles me in its impossible grease.
Stifled in word grease, in love grease
in hate grease
(in surrogate grease?)

the confusion is "catastrophic."

"Abandoned to the Powers"

In the quarry
there is scratching and screeching
and breaking and bending.
Or is it merely the circulation
of the blood, nerve impulses,
some old damage of the spine marrow?
(I am so stupid about anatomy,
is that why I am stupid about "love"?)

Once again, all is quiet.
(all lamps have been switched off)
The eyes of a half-grown girl, "my girl"
stare at me through the dark.

How does it feel in her eyes?
How does she — in the dark —
experience the color pink?
(In what way does it hurt her?)

Do I "love" her?

I wanted to talk with her about "love."
I wanted to talk with her about "suffering."

My joints are swollen
dark blotches cover my skin

but my fingernails stay where they are.

I wanted to show her a way.

I do not know a way.
(I put one foot in front of the other)

I wanted to talk with her about "sharing."
(my cheeks are free from shadow
but the big dog is keeping watch)

"Love"
"The most beautiful word in the language"

(how do you understand, just now, the expression "beautiful"?)

No, I do not know any way out of this,
I am stuck in it
(I nail myself to it)

like the skeletal woman in her slatted cage

whom the hungry ape claws
through the sun-fragrant hair.

"Love"?

Soon the white coffin is lowered.
The larks are "almost bursting with song,"
the clover is "flying its flags."
It is a very "beautiful" day.
A beautiful day full of "love,"
of "love's sorrows"
two small bareheaded children
with sun-fragrant hair
a small church whose bell
brittly pierces the love drone.

Behind them stand those dressed in black,
those waiting.
(I think of myself,
of whom else?)

"Love."
The word "love."
It exists (for me)
but what does it mean?
(I know little about semantics,
is that why I am stupid about "love"?)

You bend over me
and my heart almost "breaks."

Is it any of that?

(Soon over)

A strange language
unknown bodies
(but what use would it be if I "understood,"
if I "knew")

You bend over me
(in my fantasies?)

The shadow bends over me
(in my fantasies?)

the incorruptible shadow
with his demands for "love"
for constancy
for betrayal
for soil.

(What do you think about when you think about "love"?)

What a question!

You sit in front of me
on the empty (?) chair.
The chair is blue, with black stripes.
(What do you think about the color blue,
this color almost turquoise but more blue
and with a pattern of black stripes
like some kind of—black!—straws
or stylized black swallows.)

The upholstery is "rough"
with raised threads.

How does it affect you?

What inner taste, "emotional color"
do you experience when confronted with the rough,
black-patterned, turquoise (but more like blue)
upholstery material
of that chair?

You aren't even here.

(the chair isn't even here)

When you come in
and switch on the weak bulb
I am already asleep

dreaming about my forgotten cigarettes
or about the yellow (cool cool yellow)
flowers on the heath.

Or I remember.
With my taste I remember.

My time does not coincide with your time.
(How do you experience—just now—the concept time?)

I "love" you.

I would so much like to say that I "love" you.
(and nothing is "true" or "false")
But how can I get through to you
or, more "truly" (?)
to my image of you?

(and what difference would it make if I could?)

I would so much like to call you "dear."
(how many haven't I called "dear")
And always with different nuances
with different "contents"
(or lack of content)

How do you understand (how did you experience,
as a child) the concept
"content"?

I would so much like to call you "dearest."
(how many haven't I called dearest)

I walk across the meadow.
It is damp.
It feels sick
like a melancholic hymn.

I let my feet sink in between the tussocks.

The mushrooms are unfolding.

The blotches are unfolding.
on the skin
(and on the "inner skin")

Come.

Is that so?

Come.

(to how many haven't I shouted "come")
And always with a different intensity,
different nuances,
different tones
or lack of tone.

Come!

You walk away from me
disappear

my image of your image
grows weaker
disappears

recedes
like my cry.

Come!

I red.

The wind is cold.

(but only the monotonous heath)

"Love"?

Come!

The wind is cold.

Come!

(but only shadow
darkness
soil)

The "beloved" girl's eyes
(like yours!) so pained.

(Of whom do you think when you hear the word "pained"?)

I know no way.

I still walk (stand sit lie) in the mess
in the trash (in my fantasies?)
picking
putting back
"clearing."

I'll have to go on until I die.

The mushrooms swell
but are soon gone.

Soon the girl walks in the sun
and talks about "love."

(Does she yearn for the sunshine?
Does she yearn for the sweet grass?
Does she yearn for the green color

with a dash of poison

the graveyard color?)

Soon the girl walks in the sun and talks about "love."
Soon she will be immersed in its warm grease:
sunshine grease, sharing grease, understanding grease,
grief grease, etc. etc.

The funeral procession traverses the village once again

(or the city: there, less "expressively"
less "sentimentally")

A black coffin, this time.
Black automobiles, worming
their way through the messy traffic.

The grief, finding its various "expression":
"petrified" "blowsy" "acidulous" "insipid"
(or, on other occasions, concerning other "subjects")
"constrained" "admirable."

(how are you affected by the black traffic?)

"Love"?

The lamp is out.
We sit "together" at the table.

Yet awhile.

You call my name
as long as you feel like it.
I answer
(answer?)

—and always with different nuances,
different contents—
as long as I feel like it.

We do not know what we are calling.
We do not know whom we are answering.

"A little love is all I desire"
let him give it who can.

(Then there are other sweet numbers
    such as
"Alone with my shadow"
    or
"Where is the friend I'm seeking everywhere"
    or
"I can't give you anything but love")

As long as I feel like it.

The anthill has grown over me.

The rats are over me
as long as they feel like it.

"Love"?

Your blotchy skin, your nails
rotting among the mushrooms.

(But I hold on.
I scratch and scrabble a hold.)

I do have my cigarettes.
I do have (e.g.) my bathrobe.
I "love" my bathrobe.
It is red.

(What do you think of the color red,
the nuances between tomato red and bloodred?)

"My heart bleeds"
my joints swell

but my fingernails stay on.

"Suffering" —
I know it well
my suffering, who else's

and only from time to time.

"My death is mine"
My fingernails stay where they are.

Before I know it, I am "well."
(my joints do not hurt anymore)

The spots on my skin
are "just a memory."

The old woman in her cage
(surely I "love" her?)
is "just a memory"

The hands
that bent mine backward
at an unnatural painful angle
(surely I "love" them)
are "just a memory."

Surely I "love" you.
Does that mean anything to you?

(and what difference would it make
if it did)

The funeral procession goes through the village
(or through the city) again
and the hymns are sung
sick, melancholic —
dissolved in the violently rising wind.

I stretch "voluptuously."
I stretch and yawn.

You are gone.

The old woman is gone.

The ape that tore the child's hair.
The girl "my loved one" closes her eyes in the sun.

I huddle up, feeling "voluptuous."
I curl up and yawn.

"Love"?
I know nothing about "love."
(I know nothing about "suffering")

I close my eyes behind my pink walls.
I hear a lot of words.
"music" "dog" "shadow" "soil"
"sharing" "content" "indescribable"

TOBIAS BERGGREN

As a fiery if not too easily accessible cultural critic, Tobias Berggren (b. 1940) has reconciled Marxist and structuralist trains of thought. He has attacked the demand for "simplicity" and "accessibility" that according to him have watered down a great deal of recent Swedish poetry. In Berggren's view, this trend does not represent anything new, but is merely a relapse into a simplistic, premodernistic consciousness. Since reality no longer is simple, it cannot be the function of art to have people standing around mouthing platitudes, even if that is what they do in "real life." This is an overly simplified outline of some of Berggren's points of attack.

Det nödvändiga är inte klart (The Necessary Is Not Clear) is the title of Berggren's first book, published in 1969. The thesis of the book is that new ideas are linguistically unclear. The language of the old society, the old oppression, the old ideas, lingers on and influences our concepts. For new ideas to become clear, they first must transform the language. "The day follows upon night, the world, upon words."

Berggren's poetry is firmly rooted in the academic modernistic tradition. In later collections his own voice and reality are more prominent, the books no longer weighed down by long discourses on language. In them, Berggren *performs* the linguistic and historical consciousness he mostly *talked* about previously. Although arguing against many of the 1960s' New Simplistic catchphrases, Berggren in his poems carries on the political commitment that characterized the decade.

Lynäs, a Quartet

≪*Translated by Lennart Bruce*≫

I

29th of August, late evening, we arrive at the house in Norrland
I try to make a fire in the stove, it won't work, the chimney is
                                                                smoking

But I persist, the kitchen fills with smoke and you disappear
I get tired and my eyes water, but I want the fire! I persist

in lighting it, in writing two-line stanzas, playing the piano, cooking,
marinating herring and making love, and out there within the
                                                masses of leaves in the dark

the sleeping larvae bite their cocoons in their dreams,

and Gilgamesh walks with the light through night's mountain
feeding on the dark during his extended journey

It has to work! Lighting a fire, to stop that damned tennis
                                                                match, to
reinstate socialism in Chile, to crush imperialism, it'll work

I insist, I defend the dangling cocoons, ancient myths
                                                and you persisting
in the smoke, I've lived for a while now, I know:

Together we create the light and light is the food of the earth,

the earth devours it out there in the night, and even the
                                        stones in the dark
the glances of the gray zones, will barely let go of it

while the dark blades of grass nod knowingly, hinting
                                        at the stillness
the one where everything travels faster than light . . .

And fires in iron stoves aren't so much for the sake of the heat
                                        when there are
radiators, nor for the cooking, when there are electric hot plates,

No, fires in stoves are for conversation's sake and the toil
of lighting them; the human

light that one creates

                        II

Together we create the light . . .
The stars are there before us with their brightness, in the eyes
                                        of scorpions, and yet
we do create it; the language
moves in the light
like a pollen grain
in motionless water . . .

And if man eats light he disintegrates . . .

The shadows of the seagulls on the snow and the reflection
                                        of the child's body
over there on her closed eyes and your
eyes on the portrait above the typewriter . . . :

the language moves in the light; visible movement apparent
telling of the invisible, real,
indiscernible movement impossible without eyes,
perceivable and unperceived motion
growing together,
grains of pollen fertilize plants and
growing fruits pump the quiet
water into the plant,

the water where the stars are reflected,
starlight with cut roots . . .
But out of the water come
the slow shovings of the whales
against the polar ice, fetuses, new thoughts
and swiftness . . .
          silence and time . . .
      quick whispers and weapons . . .

          III

                    . . . quick rustling steps
the vanished people of the woods;
I saw them once
in the shadow-play of leaves against a wall
in some trivial situation, waiting for a bus

You were there!
you had been there . . .
your hands were so familiar

But what were we chasing . . . ? The
heavy earth, in its hot absence, turns speechless,
not even the ice ages can master that, in spite of
our changing of species and we're still changing
between us,
and what does time mean —

The ancient hunters in the woods
hand me your eyes here
frightened . . . And
later at night . . .

In our shadow plays we chase the earth
the animal of light with a transparent beak
holding our bodies in its scream

IV

The smoke has been cleared
and I barbecue three whitefish, think of whatever I feel like,
sit looking at the fire, energy is indestructible and the work
creates us

now I hear your steps, you're coming back, come here and sit down
in the warmth, I love you, the smoke is gone,

and eyes dry, come let's sit here
and talk while the cocoons
sing in the dark
songs that eat darkness, come let's sit down
and eat fish broiled on the open fire in our world on earth

V

Swinging cocoons, sleep and moss . . .
the moss
and the hyphae, the semidead mating—
correspondences that
develop without prayers
without waste, the roots of the moss and

the death of the moss, the bitter
roots of the heather and the death of the heather,
the twigs from which the berries fall
unpicked
in crowded fertilization
the moist overpopulated earth

The spores of the mushrooms and of the moss
and the club moss's search for
its needless butterfly, the message of the moss
and waterlogged correspondences
inexorable and invisible
there deep in the forest . . .

In there where no man
set his foot on the ground
never planted by humans but forever
sowed by light . . .

There in the forest I live
in you

as a butterfly embryo
    aching in its cocoon
        swinging from that tree
            that no god hears tumble
when it falls in the storm
    on the damp earth's
        implacable regrowth . . .

Light has no ears—
But governs the winds!

A Summer Evening at Slite

≪*Translated by Gordon Brotherston and Gunnar Harding*≫

One evening we drive out to see the lights
of the cement factory on the other side of the bay
We see them mirrored in the water, and the factory seems to us
somehow to grow bigger
Maybe it's the surprising contrast
with the rural landscape, it's as if
an enormous industrial city lay there, as if suddenly
we stood on the shore of an alien and dirty river
maybe in the Ruhrgebiet or North Italy or the Urals . . .
On the water the wind delineates the signs
of unseen traffic
And the signs of our experience ask us
why we refuse to be where we are

In the ash trees above us the midges whine
The high unvarying note holds hard and firm
Like a transformer in an alien factory plant, barren
and scorched in the siesta hours, oil stains
on the concrete and whitewash flaking off the walls
under the mesh of drainage pipes . . .
And through the ash trees' mesh, trunks, roots
the processes of darkness get connected
with the water of the bay
its surface is wrested and dissolved
by the lights from an unknown city in the darkness of the brain,
where in the glow of a streetlamp under an unknown constellation
a passerby asks for a match
this evening that glimmers in passing as we walk here

And we are the interstices in the places we inhabit
which other worlds permeate, and our footprints
on the ground under the ash trees are the signs
of our presence somewhere else

Where does this place lie in the darkness? What shall happen to us
with our love? Do our experiences portend
a true shift? Far out to see
on the rails of longitude
fearful forces shunt
Europe's landscape into one: A world
where there's nothing left to know, where differences are ironed out
where human beings are effaced from their places. A world
without presence, where we, indifferent to the peculiarities of the
world,
lose it . . .

But under our feet the chalk plunges to the crystal flow . . .
The secret worlds of the hill stratum after stratum under the earth
Caves of transparent stalactites
and blind white bats that live imprisoned deep down, a thousand
yards
under the shallow waters of the bay, with shrunken eyes, dreaming
they circle inside the mountain through the cracks, ceaselessly
testing their position with inaudible sound . . .
And a presence exists
As in a landscape where under a million stones that
you can turn up
you hear a barely audible music, which stops abruptly

A landscape
whose inhabitants, anxious
but friendly, stamp
a sign on your wrist: "Go on
toward your inaudible speech! . . ."

We leave, the small car takes us across worlds
that still are ours within,
through the Night Mountain

Song of Time, at the Sea

≪Translated by Lennart Bruce≫

I

A seal hunter moves
underneath my shadow across the limestone rock
slowly on his way to vanish
toward the roots of the stars
I am his shadow
in the light from the blue fire

And the light of the sea, of the water
that filters all relationships with a quiver, dissolves
the hard dependencies of the earth into pelagic fantasies,
vegetating frequencies, the schools of herring
expanded dreaming vagrant songs
for the bones of the drowned
spelling the sign for Relationship
The light of the sea
that throws my shadow against the stars

What wave brought me here? That of the drowning one?
The wave of the one already drowned; reflecting the constellation
    of Pisces —
was at least visible, that wave
was only for one of us; "that one is for me," and
he takes a deep breath, "it was never to be she" and sinks
with the boat, is eaten
and destroyed;
the atom furnaces
of the fish-stars
open in his brain,
eel, cod-spawn are now sightseeing
the broken eyes of bone —

You there, in the sign of the Angler
take into consideration
you, with the algae in your heart, your summer winds, consider
that here lies someone
who was once five years old too
who picked cones and cloudberries in the pine woods
who was five years of age and stood at the bottom of the food
                                                            chain
Now a tenderly experienced human creature
is eaten
by currents and mollusks
Now the human being is being eaten

Now, sitting there under the surfaces of the photos
at a face of stone
which mercilessly portrays
a frightened, scared to death
species, unknown
dourly and dangerously inscrutable . . .
The fowls of the sky keep watch

                    II

The clock ticks, the waves of the sea and the rustling leaves
of the trees on the beach
move in life, and its screams and songs
rock through my head
Time has run out, is the work done? Never
did I think so little
could be accomplished in so long a time, the leaves
do more and ruin nothing

The clock sings its absolute song
for the trees that sway in the wind from the work of men
Time is not like the clock
Time is uneven, and full of energy
as it is scattered
among the humans, we grope for it with clicks and wheels as
we grope for the day and the light with doors and windows and
    fingers, but
we spill the world
in the alchemy of retention

In the alchemy of return we devastate the world

Because all is movement and movement changes
and not the swallows, the electrons or the agile weeds
or the decaying societies or
the Medusa-shaped blotch of humidity on the wall of the
                        summerhouse
nor the exploding stars nor you
are reality
beyond the web of relationships swaying
back and forth for screams and songs, the time out there
is in the heart of a dog or in the roots of the ocean-floor mountains
or anywhere and myriad, but the stars
rotate on shafts of human matter, and the oceans
can do nothing without the peoples of their shores, and the
                        fishermen
nothing with their nets without symbols and the nets
of relationships nothing
with the sound scales of the clock
strewn about
on the grass where the children play

The grass can split an atom furnace
but man can never start over again

III

The inventory of the shore
among its properties are also human bodies
This broken home —
You walked up to me on the beach, I was full of joy . . .
you left me: a shore
from which we're led away irrevocably, from which
my body disappears with the tide
Oh, I stood turned facing the sea
the whole front of my body lit by the light of the horizon, and
my back in hell
Do you see my back in the dark?
Here it is, here in what I've written
here
At the place where I write of the memory of you

I looked all over this limestone rock and found
the rusty iron nail
where you hurt yourself
Your blood was still there
Yellow lichens had grown in it

LARS FORSSELL

Lars Forssell (b. 1928) began his career writing poems replete with cultural allusions and references to esoteric poets. He had spent some time in the United States and had translated Ezra Pound, whose work had considerably influenced his own. He had also lived in Paris and returned home with impressions of French cabaret songs, rendering a number of them into Swedish. Accompanying the main body of his work are chansons, often bitter, sardonic, and politically pointed. Forssell's close ties to the world of the theater and the political cabaret have left their mark on his poetry. He excels at the "persona" poem and is, perhaps, at his best when expressing himself through a mask: he has written sequences on Nijinsky, Lenin, Lenny Bruce, and others.

"What's the use of 'protesting' here in Sweden? If you do, you just run the risk of being interviewed by *Veckojournalen*," Forssell once stated. (*Veckojournalen* is a large-circulation glossy weekly with "class" aspirations.) Yet he has protested: he was one of the first Swedish writers to condemn United States involvement in Vietnam. He has also become notorious for more personal and impulsive attacks on, for instance, Swedish hereditary nobility, opera singer Birgit Nilsson, and actors who did margarine commercials. *Veckojournalen* has, indeed, interviewed him, and he was elected to the Swedish Academy, another institution he has satirized.

To critics who claim that his poems are too charming, private, theatrical, Forssell replies: "There has to be room in the poem for the whole human being. You know—they say that Tchaikovsky is sentimental, messy, full of bathos: but if you could remove exactly those flaws, you wouldn't have Tchaikovsky any longer. And I *like* Tchaikovsky."

Mariage avec Dieu

≪*Translated by Anselm Hollo*≫

1

They all stopped talking
when Romola opened the door
There was something in the air, she thought
like the big bird on the wing
himself, in flight, the famous
crevade, in slow motion

2

"What is it?"
Berthe's beet-red fingers
stood still in the dough
Marcello said "Niente"
but Heinz came out with it:
"When I was a boy
I was often sent out on errands
for Herr Nietzsche
and toward the end
he acted just like Herr Nijinsky does now"

3

She caught up with him in the village street
He was wearing the heavy gold crucifix over his tie
stopping everybody and exhorting them
to make absolutely sure they went to Mass
Romola grabbed him "That is enough
enough of that Tolstoy nonsense
You're making a fool of yourself"

4

"But my dear Romola, the world's eyes are upon me
The women are copying my costumes
They're painting their eyes aslant
because I happened to be born
with these high cheekbones
It is I, even more than Chanel
who determines the era's fashions
Why should I not try to start this new fad:
to seek the Truth?"

5

He called this his marriage to God
Married to God, he said he was

6

Very soon after they took him to the clinic in Zurich
condemned in his absence
in contumaciam

7

To quote the Professor
"Either he is insane
or *simply* Russian"
To quote the Americans
"He was crazy all right"

"Whispering, they gather round
I can hear my muscles talking
in little squeaks in
the chair I'm sitting on
They flock around
les comtes et les comtesses
clouds of perfume
or water bugs on the brown pond at Mazr
Quelles fesses!
Such opulence!

"I turn my back to them

"But now there is this horrible stench
I mustn't cry now
Down there on my wrist a muscle opens
a mouth, a little child's mouth!
You'll dance tonight
In a stench of Chanel you'll dance tonight
Dance like a rose

"Then I whisper back to my wrist
In a little while
I'll dance in a little while
in a year, in millions of years
but all they want to do is close their eyes.
For millions of years.
Dance, dance myself hard, a hard-on.
Dance the War for you, with no arms.
Explode in midair, so my guts fly out!
The War, the war you did nothing about."

Then, he danced them the War,
and no one had seen anything like it,
before, or ever since.
The lady at the piano,
notes Romola, tried to keep up with him
bravely, and to the best of her ability.

I Sleep in You

≪Translated by Anselm Hollo≫

I sleep in you
You can't know that
Close to birth I sleep
Close to enchantment

You turn in bed
Like a pregnant whale
Like wide-eyed plankton
I doze inside you

I love you
You'll never know that
Close to death I sleep
Bursting my shells

Dedication

≪Translated by Anselm Hollo≫

On my way from New York in '48
A blizzard
Six children on a sled
The train ran over

Called you in Chicago
Talked about it
What else was there to talk about
But you couldn't come

Rang
Like six scared bells
Later wrote a poem on the train
Using the words of others

Double Flute was your name then
Wind in dawn's hourglass
And echo
And all such things

You went under me then my love
Over me you came
Six heavy
Screeching wheels

Van Gogh's Ear

≪Translated by Lennart Bruce≫

Van Gogh cuts off his ear
he wraps it in a towel
slowly colored red
and sends it
to you

What are you doing with this evidence
of love madness sorrow?
Do you throw it with disgust into the flames
of your fireplace?

Or into the garbage can
Or do you hide it covertly, perhaps a little proudly
In a little box?

It seems to me
As though this ear still exists
Listening
Forever hearing
The light from the cruel cornfields

And the static from the remorseless sun.

The Chameleon

≪*Translated by Gunnar Harding and Frederic Will*≫

Stieg Trenter has told me
that when Garvis Carlsson's son
four years old then, now Garvis Jr.
the star in A.I.K.,
now Sirius,
came to Madrid where his daddy
got a job as a soccer player
he said after a year had passed
something like this:
Last year nobody talked like me
Now everybody talks like me.

Don't therefore think
that the chameleon sees himself as
a defenseless victim of his environment

On the contrary he thinks
that everything is a victim
of his own changing personality.
The world around changes with him.

He raises one of his eyebrows
and says:
"Leaves, e.g., take their greenness
from me.
The poppy takes its poppy red
from my circulatory system.

The yellow straw on the cabin's roof
flames so yellow in the sun
because I happen to have rested for a while
on the cabin's roof."

≪Translated by Gunnar Harding and Anselm Hollo≫

Are you looking for a seeing-eye dog,
man with the white cane?
Shoot your faithful sheep dog, go out in the woods
and call his wiser relation
Call the wolf, you poor bastard,
he has a fine nose for danger,
whites of eyes for ambush!
Take the wolf to help you through the city streets
and you, cripple without arms and legs,
harness a wolf to your pitiful cart

Dogs are for princes who hunt,
as is the falcon, under his hood:
The wolf on a leash, the vulture on the shoulder
are for those they hunt.

≪Translated by Gunnar Harding and Anselm Hollo≫

Who does not remember Noah and the dove
that returned with an olive branch in its beak?
But who among laymen
remembers that he sent out a raven first?

What did the raven see?
He looked and found what he was looking for:
Nothing.

Nothing but drifting corpses
ships without oars, water, decay.
That was the raven's message.

And today, Saturday, he brought word
of a bunch of ragged humans,
old ones, young women, children
being herded along the trails by soldiers
away, or home, home, or away from home,
not knowing which.

Tanguy

≪*Translated by Gunnar Harding and Anselm Hollo*≫

I

"Through a flock of birds, through fire
but through glass, never"
the useless light
that does not shine on anything
or for anyone
just shines

and the silken tuning fork
with an inaudible k

But enjoy, nevertheless, the poison-green sky
and outlined against it, splayed hands
not grasping anything
nor raising anything
just upraised

II

The prodigal son never returns
The prodigal son never returns
The prodigal son never returns
The prodigal son never returns
First version Second version
Third version Fourth version
The fifth, sixth, and seventh
still in process

Därför
Parce que
Therefore

Wild Rabbits

≪*Translated by Gunnar Harding and Anselm Hollo*≫

I

I stand here, the fire-smoke swirling around me
at the edge of the cliff
and the reflection of my face
is a jellyfish in the swell

I am in a hurry, so many things I want,
I want to go now, at dawn

I am in a hurry, I tell you,
and the world around and inside me
is standing still
and behind me, the fire is getting closer

II

In Australia, it happened:
a forest fire spread
by wild rabbits, fleeing,
small leaping torches,
a comb of fire
down their backs.

Thus fear and terror
continuously leap through the world
spreading fiery contagion.

They run under crackling branches
through the droning forest on fire
across the field to the edge of the next forest
lighting up
and setting fire to a grove on the way

The courier of terror
with the torch of fear
which we will have to put out
without ourselves going up in smoke . . .

III

The fire
does not frighten us
it must be used

the fire in the heart
the flame in your eyes

The fire of dawn, and the muzzle-fire

Tend it
Guard it
The life-flame, the fire of hope

Do you see the glow
at the edge of the charring page?

It, too, must be used.

GÖSTA FRIBERG

Gösta Friberg (b. 1936) published in his first book, *Furia* (Fury), 1964, a poem about a salmon who "in a long glide out of three years of ocean darkness" proceeds upstream: it is an appropriate image for Friberg's own development. From the start he has pursued an independent course in his work. His credo is emphatically pro-life, yet the ground-bass of his work is almost always somber. In recent years Friberg has with increasing frequency and intensity taken up ecological subject matter, to some extent influenced by the work of Gary Snyder and by Native-American poetry. He has traveled widely in the United States and Mexico, and in 1973 he published a weighty anthology of Native-American myths, poems, and visions, titled *We Shall Live Again*.

"Politically, I have come full circle: from petrified Marxism to dissolute anarchism and back again, to a nascent anarcho-syndicalism, based on ecological concern and on Martin Buber's 'I and Thou'," Friberg writes in an autobiographical note.

The long poem "Voyage through Andromeda" differs in many respects from the main body of Friberg's work. With language that he has, in part, devised, based mainly on Stockholm street talk, he creates a mystical science-fiction fantasy atmosphere—at times reminiscent of Tolkien, Scandinavian folklorists, von Däniken, and other more or less esoteric authors—from his extended and eclectic reading. The section "Dimle deppar" (1973) was intended as the opening of a long epic which has not, to date, been continued.

The Journey through Andromeda

≪Translated by Samuel Charters≫

It was early morning in Andromeda
and there where the dimmish eaves
    dribbed down from the night's fire-yellow slanting roof
stood lively little Dimle completely dragged.
The Drombs had shadowed him all night, and Starnap, who stayed
    behind his back when his pantlegs flapped around the backs
    of his knees from running,
had finished with him for a while. The caves didn't threaten him
                                                    anymore.
But over there where the mushrooms sing in fire-major and
                                                    dark-major
    he was just about to go to pieces
remembering his old life, in his worn-out cap, on earth
    on Kocksgatan.

After the pisspoor dream he'd had
    he of course pulled his peaked hood
    farther down
and thought it was over. They'd threatened to kill Death itself
    which made him catch his breath so sharply
    that he blew some life into the embers
    in the bottomless pit—and even if he did feel out of it and
                                                    down
    he still had to get his things together
which surprised him
this frosty morning.

He looked at his raggedy jeans, torn apart at the knees
with the violent physical blastoff from earth,
and since he was now about the size of a thumb
he could—with his arms akimbo—
    kick up a little morningballet
to keep warm at least. But he had the blues too bad for that.

Soon the sun should rise up through the trees.
A shadow growled, ran off and disappeared . . .

With trembling hands Dimle lit his last forestscigaret
    sat down on a stone and waited—
in dire depression he studied his brown-stained fingers
    and saw a radioactive coalfish
studying him, just as depressed, from the pool in the sylvan glade,
but right away he felt better, when he thought about Snail of the
                                        Forest Rumbo

        From his awkward little low place
Rumbo had, of course, also looked up at the night stars,
and with his pipe in his jaws and his pack frame on his back
the forest snail was one of Dimle's true friends,
    a firm one tragically thoughtful beside the fires
    he and Dimle built when they wandered together—
    cried perhaps sometimes with his lined forest-snail face
but he also was drombscarred.

"You know, Dimle," he said in his husky forest-snail's voice
and sucked thoughtfully on his pipe, "you and I are just about the
                                        last."
The dummish fire frummed, frapped and shrimmed,

Dimle warmed his hands
and the Night sank down on the peaked leather hat
that was pulled over Rumbo's head,
and he chuckled: "Also if those damned mountain cliff-tomts
    direct their deadly radar smile at everything that's living
they won't get you!" and took a berry sandwich out
    of his pack frame
and passed it to Dimle. "Eat!" he said. He saw how badly
Dimle was feeling, since all he had was a skizzy little gleam
    from his old life on earth
so he had to eat, to get through the night.

Out of their mouths stepped their breath's small shining hare shit
                                     balls
    in the chilly darkness.
They looked up above them in the night, listening: an *infinnid*,
                                infinitely distant.
as if it were streaming down from a heaven overswum in starlight.
Dimle had never seen anything like it before.
It wasn't like anything he remembered from earth.
High, clear-burning flames glimed from the depths of caves —
or juked out of the way, dribbling off like tears
    down the black sunbark's lined cheeks . . .
Out of the night's mouth, which breathed with such a distant light
that they lowered their eyes, something stepped down
    and bowed with the immense aura of colors
only found around the stealers of the sacred fire who lost their
                            way on the tundra
then glided on with their travel canes and sweaters
    knit out of the aurora borealis.
"An old space longshoreman," whispered Rumbo,
"one of the outcasts." They saw his fiery footsteps draw away
                             over the plain

"Button up your peepers," muttered Rumbo and pushed Dimle's head down, "if you flummer around out there you'll go out of your mind. Here there are some of the strangest night creepers, hags that dromb the gleam in your eye and twitter your soul away to night asylums—if you don't dummy up in time and keep your eyes on the ground."

"There goes The Tramp." Dimle followed Rumbo's pointing finger into the night sky, "his red-tinged beard is shining there because he's staring at a far-off invisible sun. One leg shorter than the other, and blind. He's carrying The Radium Field tied to the bundle on his back. The ruby-red star down there to the left is the heel of his one shoe.

And The Ruin, burning there behind The Tramp's back, a barren galaxy with crumbled walls burned down to the star foundations.

And if you tie the darkness together now between those two stars there you get a strange kind of dress, yeh? That's The Scoundrel Worm of The Pickled Jack. She's always waning and getting darker. Farther off there, when The Villain's Jealousy Swarm passes her head, then she gets a red kerchief that winds over her shoulder, and makes faces for weeks.

"Hell, the stars aren't important. It's only those there little pisswitches like you that come from earth that look at the stars. It's the room space, the space room that's misterioso. I mean the room's space is a thing that's always there. No matter where you move you have it around you, at least. You can, as an example, be without the ground under your feet, just float for a minute, but you never get out of the spacething. The stars are only the breakout space makes so it can rush out and shine the way it's supposed to. Snails know a lot about astronomy, if you check the house we build on our backs you understand the kind of harmony we move in. I certainly belong to the anarchistic forest-snail race that has a pack frame to go on my back and star-thick wino's coat to roll myself up in. But anyway. The Snail that looks out of his house is *star*, when he pulls himself in again he's *room*—room, room—star. It's always being at home in your body whichever way you turn. Dig me."

And Dimle saw how Rumbo slithered out onto the distant field to glim a little night dew as it streamed over the blue-tinged clover, dripping to the ground. And Rumbo's movements were really beautiful, a kind of rhomboid glittering where he was slithering along in the stardust between the stones, sudden snazzy small lumberings at his utmost slow snail speed, at the same time here and there holding out his leather cap and shaking the dew down from the surprised grass. He made a sudden high leap into a rowanberry and nudged down the cluster of berries, which he then with his practiced hands, smoking his pipe at the same time, squeezed into juice with the dew. He bopped a little on the way back to Dimle to give him a laugh. "Dum the dum dum dum of the dum dum" drummed Dimle on his own temple. In some curious way Rumbo's movements reminded him of the summring, rhombroid glimmerings of the spaces of the inner ear . . . "Dum dum of the dum dum."

"Quiet," said Rumbo. They heard a faraway song.
Neanderthal-tomts had already started to light their lanterns
    in the distant glen,
and Rumbo (who was an old psychewarden
who had taken the shape of a snail to follow Dimle
    on the long trip through Andromeda)
knew how dangerous it was
when the Neanderthal-tomts came out of the mountain, clearing
                                                        their
throats, drowsing, and shambling along. A single glimpse of their
                                                        faces
    could make a Black Dark Cobbler lose his teeth in the last
    and run for his life into the primordial night.

They put out the fire and crept down on the ground.
A forest rose twittered something to a red rowanberry cluster, but
it was silent again and they lay completely still. A fox went
past in his spirit clothes, around a cliff, and disappeared . . .

A little dressing down as a tomt suddenly rushed out with a lantern in his hand and jumped with both feet on everything that moved, piled bushes and brush out of the way, and behind him limned light shine; a long line of large grown creatures came walking, all of them with dangling atom lanterns in their belts.
For a moment Dimle thought they stared out petrified with terror:
    heavy heads hanging down,
big brown baggy pants, high brown wool caps
over something that wasn't a face, something that was like a
                      glowing slat
but it was too dark to see—with a jerk they started to move again.
Two half-grown, completely black clothed tomts jumped up and
                         down
along the sides to keep the line straight, jumped up in trees and
down from cliffs, jumped on the mushrooms, stamped and kicked
until their vague humming Stromboli colors were put out . . .
The ones in brown sighed and groaned under
the orders of the little black pigs.
The night itself seemed manic, on the edge of an epileptic attack,
and shone its visage shorn of power in space:
the black forest roses stopped their music in the shadows of the
    rowanberry trees
and hid their faces in their tiny hands. "Hate, hate hunger"
    thought the deep places
that felt the shuddering of the atomic torches rub over the ground
with heavy steps. "Hate, hate, hunger," cried a heap of dry
                      branches,
    jumping up
and setting fire to itself; soughing from between the tomts gapped
                      teeth:
    "Oooooh," they squeaked and shielded themselves with their
                arms, hid themselves in their armpits
and stood motionless for a moment in the gleam—
while the roots laid their foreheads in a deep seam
    and brooded under the earth—
Dimle, scared shitless, lay hidden in his furrow in the earth.

"The ones in brown are prisoners," whispered Rumbo, "the ones
in black
are Tertiary-tomts that joined up with the forbidden
to get their hands on the Neanderthal-tomts' secrets
They want to take control of the fire wildness that's in the atom
lanterns.
The ones in the brown caps must have been blasted somehow and
driven into a trap:
their arms and the upper parts of their bodies are snared in volcanic
sweaters
but they can still turn their heads. Don't look into their faces!
Don't look into their faces! Their faces kill."
But Dimle was too rocked psychologically
to get Rumbo's warning. Besides he didn't hear very well
(since his time as first drummer in "Holy Brothers").
He lay and stared into something that reminded him of gloomy
Christmas eves
on Kocksgatan,
the old folks on a drunk and the bright fire light striking in his face.

"Duck, dammit!" cried Rumbo. But before Dimle could hunker
down on the ground
one of the volcano-felled creatures started to starckel and stamp —
the firefern sat with his hands around his knees and sang in the
distance —
and a large, heavy head started to turn its face toward him . . .
Dimle got a glimpse of something horrible, terrifying, in profile
against
the stars, something that was smiling,
but still filled Dimle with such agony that he just wanted to
jump up,
scream, and strike out blindly around him, a black echo without
sound
was at his shoulder and touched it . . .
But Dimle had turned to a stone presence, his face had turned to a
stone presence

and in the next moment he was a small sparkle
that jumped up and down in the back of his own head
to avoid the heavy crash
of a face that came rushing through his brain and screamed out
his innermost echoes . . . and behind that face, which ran and
                                                        glided
in its own glow without taking form . . . he saw the group of
                                                  black tomts
that pointed in at him triumphantly—and he
spun as he jumped, at the black point of the sparkle, whose door
he slammed again
        against the wave of hammering sledge blows
that songed in against his golden—he took the elevator
fourteen thousand floors under the earth, jumped out with the
                                        shining gold flimran
        under his arm
followed by a whole dancing line of shambling volcanoes, led by
that face bolting from its own light streaks. . . . "Tommy
                                                  Thumb"
        hopped up in front of them, turned in the air
and jumped out through the back of his own head, right out into
                                        the coal black
where he flew like a woodshare over the earth, out of the way of
                                                  all hell,
        flew like a wind! with the psychic revolutionaries exploding
                                        behind their legs
until what seemed to be freedom over there took shape

        IN A BIG BLACK CALM GROWING . . . and he understood
that everything was over: an old tired voice
coaxed him out of there, said that he was in Death
and that he should come . . .
A gestalt of infrared waves, without contour, came through the
                                                  trees
cast Dimle up on its back and bore him away into the forest.

Now he stood before The Dark One.
He tried to do a few tap steps, drum on a stump, and asked if he
            got to
   smoke a last cigaret
and just when Death's hand lifted him up
feeling around his neck with bony fingers
to wring his neck with a sudden jerk
   Dimle stumbled and with his heel tore a sparkle out of Death's
            bony hand
The sparkle grew and grew, he heeled it over his head
played with it, juggled with it
   jumped with this marvelous light upon Death's rib
   that clanged and glistened under his feet.
He propped the sparkle up on Death's breast like a torch
took off his shoes and banged out a solo with them on Death's rib:
   icy, vibrating tones that little by little filled with color
And Death, who'd stretched himself out on the grass, seemed to
            be listening
   with his head in his hands and a straw in his mouth.
And Dimle, who was hopping around like a xylophonisk marimba
            player
   clanged the most wonderful tones out into the night
   on Death's powerful chest that was heaving and sinking . . .
He played with the sweat running down his head and shoulders,
            right up until he
   through the ribs, down inside Death, saw a little bent old man
   come out, sit down on a wood shelf and catch up on his
concertina
   and begin to back up from out of the depth
   with distant sorrowing tones—
They went through "The Last Rose of Summer," "Stardust,"
   with Dimle playing the harmony
and finished up with "In the Mood" with both of them
   keeping the beat in the three breaks
   and then coming in together on the last break
   with an enormous swing that made Death laugh and look up
   into the stars . . .

Suddenly it was dark.
And Death said: "I also have my longings and my subconscious.
Think how long I have to go, before I reach through
to life, when I can force my way in and really become Death—
first there, and I've wandered miles out in emptiness then, I see
first
the streams of crimsoning darkness of the growing night
that's my sunrise, that darkens everything
and that for me is the deepest beauty—and behind my back
all those tramps, all those unborn Deaths, that wandered up out of
the endlessness
without having even a single glance of the first black lights, like a
sign
that they've reached their own—perhaps just now someone who's
standing at a fork in the road
rubbing his stubbly beard and seeing the first
    lights of a house in the distance
darken toward that morning he's always been on his way to . . .
what happiness for one of those death tramps
to get to sit themselves like a bum against the wall of the house
and bask their faces in the night's zenith—to have gotten there!

To turn out the flames of the fires, the stars
people's fluttering hearts on the paths: it's our way
to come walking from the other direction—
into ways and realities, whose beauty you don't have any idea
about
and never get to see. . . . But maybe you didn't know
that we love music, just like you who live in the light,
when you play and hear the silence between the notes
that's us playing from the other side.
So I don't know if I'll kill you now
and grow a little more and get richer through your death,
but after you've played so deathly wonderful
I'm going to let you go—But keep it a secret,
since everything that's growing and insisting on even stronger
darkness

behind my back
is going to think I'm a traitor—since you don't know
what's going to happen when we, in our entropic power, succeed
in turning everything out!
I'll tell you about that some other time. Scram now.
Take this sparkle here and stick it in your hat." The sparkle
stepped
from Death's chest, circled in front of Dimle's eyes,
sat down on his ear and sang right in his face,
and those infrared waves, without contour, stepped from between
the trees
picked Dimle up by his back
and carried him out of the forest, dropped him and disappeared . . .

"Shame on you, Satan," said Rumbo, when the red torches curved
away in a ravine
and disappeared in the night.
He splashed a little dew on Dimle, who lay with his hands around
his head.
"Shame on you, Satan," said a humming fire morel, straighten-
ing her Stromboli hat and flouncing out her colors little by little in
the shadow of the trees. "We better get out of here before all hell
breaks loose again," said Rumbo and raised his head and shoulders.
"Take care of yourself and soon you'll be able to fly down to de-
partment Seven," smiled smuckly around the pipe stem and guf-
fawed without Dimle understanding why. "You really should get a
gold star." "Yes?" said Dimle, taking out his dog-eared notebook
filled only with question marks. Rumbo took a large gold star out
of his vest, licked it, and put it on with the bottoms of his knobby
hands. "Besides you had damned mazeltov to get away from that
face still alive. I only know one other that pulled through it. And
that's Blackshade. Old Blackshade in Haddrap, three miles north
of Mossy, Cometcliff. But he was a little behind after it—you're a
little behind too—but he's behind everything." They started off
toward the light that glittered at the horizon.
    A shadow popped up in ripped low shoes and stumped around
in his overcoat to keep warm. It was Blackshade. He just nodded

and kept his strange, sidelong glance on the ground, then he took hold of himself by his stubbly beard and leaned down presenting himself to Rumbo and Dimle: "Boys, read in the rag this a.m. that the keepers are on the way." They looked around. And far off in the distance they thought they could see some white dressed creatures coming closer. "We'd better haul ass out of here."

At a fast snail's pace they set out over the plain, Rumbo in the middle, Dimle on his right and Blackshade on his left, running low to the ground into the deep places . . .

They looked around again. And way behind the keepers' white dots in the distance they saw a gleam over the horizon, a little lopsided set mouth that in its hairline flicker widened out like a small shining slash between the Night's thighs. "One of their usual tricks," muttered Rumbo. The slash widened, grew, and suddenly lit up the space in such an immense, high daylight that they were forced to crawl along the ground and hold on to the boulders so they wouldn't be pulled away by the onrushing galaxy's heavy, droning spiral arms, which whirled everything up into the unbearable stillness found only in dreams . . . forests, mountains, everything was lit up and they lay flipped out as if it had been going on forever . . . and when they looked up once they stared into a glowing fingerprint that slowly spun its stardust in whirlpools . . . they thought they saw faces leaning down, faces striped in their hurry . . . before a vacuum of ultrablack waves burst the silence, took the breath out of the air, sucked up the last gasping heavy blows of wind and roared into outer space . . . and just beyond the horizon everything stood quiet again, like a spinning fire sea clambering on its spiral arms . . . before its shine stopped again diminishing and far beyond itself, in a whirling, flickering motion . . . that was drawn up out of the invisibility . . . and from the last little hairs of light on their way for all time into the darkness they thought they heard a voyagers' song . . .

"The Great Proleton!" cried Rumbo, and ran after it with impetuous snail movements, shading the peak of his cap with both hands. "The proletariat's own flaming galaxy that only shows up once every thousand years!" They stared at a stone that began to stir at their feet, a stone that seemed to be whining deep within its glowing point, as if it wanted to lift itself from the ground. But it couldn't, as Rumbo expressed it, palarch its heavy stoneset and get a slow stoneflight to join up with its origin in the flowing starmass that disappeared at the horizon . . . it rolled over a few times on the ground, gave up and went on sipping at its stonebeer and staring into its stone TV, until it went to sleep with its head down on its stone hand.

They ran again, in the direction of the disappearing gleam, whose last hairline flicker seemed to wave in the distance. . . . "It moves so fast because it's so enormously happy in space and it was so long ago that it left its more sluggish and cosmically more bound comrades behind. What a life they have up there, going so fast they're always in the light! Even if it's night. Though I don't know anything about that kind of night. When it's night there everyone walks around in a continuous morning glow. How do they do it?" said Rumbo and slumped down into a kind of frumming, brooding silence. And now, when the light waves reached down through the darkness, the song sounded louder, the voyagers' song in the distance . . . Leaflets tumbled down into Dimle's hands, but it was too dark to read them and he stuffed them into his back pocket. (He'd get into them the first crapper he came to in Andromeda. But were there crappers? Does shitting exist in this psychy strange picture of the world.)

Suddenly he was depressed again. Off there where the light's shine disappeared only a little star was gleaming in the late night and that was the Milky Way. "To think you could take a psych rocket back there tomorrow morning," he said to himself. But he knew it was impossible. He looked at the star and thought he could make out the weak sound of the bells from Sophia Church, at an infinite distance, and suddenly he saw the kitchen table where he usually sat and read in the evenings while the rain poured down and the chimneys smoked outside in Kocksgatan's darkness. Once he'd been sitting straight up and down in that nail's point of light going by bus to Shipsbridge. And he felt all at once that he'd

been something else before, before he was Dimle, a little slimsy slit
out of something bigger, that managed to rush off in its peaked
cap before everything went under for him.

And when he saw the decayed crust on Blackshade's overcoat
an old poem came to mind, a poem he wanted to be able to write
all over Blackshade's back, split low shoes, sprunk smile and lost
eyes. A poem he loved and knew by heart and that made the
whole earth, lock stock and barrel, and their running bodies get
even deeper down under the night.

"Night, the dreaming one, so near at hand and filled with so
                      vast a number of stars
without a thought for us, distant, marvelous,
Shining there, a stranger in human guise,
high over the mountain's crown, sorrowing, with mighty
                      luster."

And the night above them was magically beautiful. It was like
Blackshade's face, with a feebleminded crease in his forehead and
a smiling strackle of goldflammer in his lower jaw when he looked
over Rumbo's head and with a total, tragic seriousness asked:
"You got any bread? I get paid on Tuesday." They were running
all this time. But Dimle shook his head. He didn't even have a
dime in his pockets.

The light was close now. And suddenly he saw Blackshade's
face go up and down and Rumbo's body slowly spiraling upward
in the air, in a whirlwind that pulled them into speechlessness . . .

Into there? into speechlessness? Or also to be lost for good
out there in a golden crash of sleep like a bundle
under the unknowable's ragged stars.

LARS GUSTAFSSON

Lars Gustafsson (b. 1936) has a solid academic background and holds degrees in philosophy from both Uppsala and Oxford. During the last fifteen years he has been one of the most prominent personalities in Swedish cultural life as a tireless debater and commentator, editor of the literary magazine *BLM*, critic, poet, novelist, author of travel journals, and playwright. Gustafsson is an indefatigable traveler: he always seems to be on his way somewhere —to Australia, Berlin, Macedonia, or Texas.

Gustafsson's poems combine a close-focus precision of detail, reminiscent of old etchings, with an awareness of the fantastic in life: logic and imaginative play intertwine throughout his work, and there is always a fresh breeze blowing, making the bizarre old vehicles rise into the sky. Writing about Jules Verne, one of his favorite authors, Gustafsson says: "There is a touch of paradoxical irony to this oeuvre, apparently so dedicated to a kind of energetic de-mystification, yet constantly winding up in the realm of the fantastic." That would seem to apply to Gustafsson as well. The high incidence of curious trivia in his poetry does not prevent him from being an intellectual who is centrally involved in the actual and ideological arguments of his day.

Lately, Gustafsson's interest in complex and ingenious mechanisms has led him to the sonnet, the sestina, and other intricate verse forms, and he has mastered them with great delicacy and elegance.

The Wright Brothers
Arrive at Kitty Hawk

≪*Translated by Gunnar Harding and Frederic Will*≫

In an excited dream I saw everything clarified:
ceremoniously Otto Lilienthal floats in his glider

down the steep hill near Grosslichterfelde.
A violent wind blew, as for kites,

and someone talked monotonously about "the gnostic darkness."
It was a warning, a whispering which came and went.

Bakunin boards the freighter Andrew Steer,
one spring day, in the harbor of Nikolayevsk, amid shacks and
                                                    sheds.

In the nineteenth century the sea often smells stale in calm.
The Revolutions are prepared. The *seafire* sparkles

And Milton Wright, Bishop in the United Brethren Church,
gave Wilbur and Orville one of Pénaud's models:

not unlike a deformed bird with a hungry neck.
Wind tunnel experiments by the warehouse of the bicycle factory

and the dry sand smoking in stubborn wind.
What is good and evil for a kite? It flutters,

rises in a steep rush but with a dead movement
in the moment it was to sever its line,

the too short line. In Africa the locomotives rust.
And the steamship *Savannah* with fluttering pennants

over the unreal blue of the sea. Solemn smoke.
Nature is always obvious: the aileron and the propeller.

Dresden, Hanoi. And the "gnostic darkness."

The Balloon Travelers

≪*Translated by Gunnar Harding and Frederic Will*≫

Look at the tall man over there in the top hat.
He is leaning out observing westward.
It is early in the morning, echoing light.

The town is awaiting in the distance with its bells
The peaks of the towers cast blue shadows innocently
It is completely calm, the moment before departure.

From nearby the balloon is huge, like a giant pumpkin
it is shining and growing, it is multicolored.
And the murmur from the spectators, a swarm of bumblebees,

They are cheering and waving at the travelers in the basket,
who pretend not to notice and keep silent about their destination.
They are immovable and ready to depart.

The man in the top hat is still observing,
and he raises the spyglass of shining brass
as if he were looking for clouds or something invisible.

When they rise they will diminish to a point
until they reach the highest air strata and snow,
the whitest snow cooling and dazzling

will fill the air they breathe, touch their foreheads.
In autumn you can see it fall as frost
the heights' breath fumbling over the fields,

and some autumn when the frost falls early
you will suddenly remember them and their trip
and how they still are climbing, as in dizziness higher

through a thinner air than that of winters
with a tone like that of splintering glass
from deep forests of frailest rain.

And how they rise higher and higher through the years
till memory itself is singing frail as glass,
—and it is unbearable, forget me, believe something else:

a pleasure-trip, an adventure for connoisseurs!
A gentleman there in light cutaway with bright-blue vest
gives a slow signal with a gloved gesture.

It is free and already it rises,
imperceptible the cheering sinks below.

"The Perfectionists'" Colony in Oneida, N.Y.

≪*Translated by Thomas Vance and Vera Vance*≫

Innumerable shadows populate this world:
the voices of men, women, sucklings
small as the crickets under the trees.

Nobody can see this country and not love it

In large abandoned white rooms in a gigantic house
there was a surprising hundred-year-old fragrance
as from unfamiliar white bread or wood.

The white church has struck its twelve o'clock
and at an altitude of 30,000 feet, soundless
and visible only as a streak of mist,

the plane from Montreal to Boston.
In 1848: bankruptcies and flyleaves,
smithies no longer in operation and a house under tall elms:

for thirty years hundreds of men and women lived here
in total sexual and economic communion:
they kept glass shops, silversmithies and a new order of things

There are still traces of the glass shops here and there,
particularly thick, opaque shards.
A fragrance of acid white wood lingers from their community.

Alexander Bryan Johnson, Jefferson, John Noyes.
They all have the same kind of steelgrey, wise eyes.
Their images pursue me in my dream:

I dream that their guilt or innocence
is my innocence or share in the world.
There is no road that takes us out of history.

And Mr. T. in his white house with high pillars tells
about the woods by the Adirondacks in 1790 and the American
                                                    brook trout:
"a lively little fellow that you only find in very clear waters"

The Machines

≪*Translated by Yvonne Sandstroem*≫

Some came early, others late,
and outside the time where it exists
each one of them is homeless.

Hero's steam ball. The voltaic pile. The ballista.
Polhem's ore hoist at Falun. Curiosities:
The "pneumatic fan."

Una machina per riscaldare i piedi.

We only perceive machines as homeless
when they belong in another century.
Then they become obvious, they acquire *meaning*.

What do they mean? No one knows.

The crankshaft device: a way of transmitting
power over long distances with the aid
of two levers moving backward and forward.
What does the crankshaft mean?

DIE BERGWERKE IM HARZ ANNO 1723

The picture teems with people. People
small as flies go up and down in the buckets,
the object marked "J" in the picture, "La Grande Machine,"
by the fresh waterfall, drives all the cables.

No one has ever combined—
as would be perfectly possible—
crankshaft and steam engine,
Voltaic pile and Hero's ball.
The possibility remains.

A foreign language that no one has spoken.

And actually:
Grammar itself is a machine
which, from innumerable sequences
selects the strings of words for intercourse:
"The healthy instruments," "the productive parts,"

"the cries," "the muffled whispers."

When the words have vanished grammar's left,
and it's a machine. Meaning *what?*
No one knows. A foreign language.
A totally foreign language.
A totally foreign language.
A totally foreign language.

The picture teems with people. Word,
small as flies go up and down in the buckets
and the object marked "J," "La Grande Machine,"
by the fresh waterfall, drives all the cables.

Brief Treatise on Seeing and Being Seen

≪*Translated by Yvonne Sandstroem*≫

Together with a half-blind sleeping dog
in a boat slowly drifting over the shoals at Entra

and some late summer waves under a warm gray sky
rattling the gravel as they break over the shoals at Entra.

And so I'm alone with the screeching gulls
who're no concern of mine, and with the memories,

the hopes, the voices, the faces of people
I've seen once and who've seen me

or the faces of those who've frightened me
who may have seen something special to frighten them.

And the feeling that somewhere I'm burning
like a salamander in the fire, somewhere I'm freezing

like a burbot in the ice, and they're both me.
And they won't merge, those pictures,

because pictures never want to merge,
so perhaps it's better without pictures;

and I remember the faces of German students
emerging from tear gas clouds, Berlin, 1968,

wearing expressions I didn't quite understand,
there was something they'd forgotten to tell me;

and from the prison at Ramleh I remember the Arab prisoners
walking round and round inside the barbed wire, three by three

looking at me ironically with wise brown eyes,
at me not at the guards or at the officers behind me,

only at me, and it was a moment of truth,
but I don't know what kind of truth;

and the gulls cry indifferently, hungrily,
drawing on the blackboard autumn has put up,

and it might be just before it rains or thunders,
or just before nothing in particular,

and when J., whom I hadn't seen for a long time,

said to me, It's impossible to love you,
it's impossible to love anyone, impossible,

there was a moment when she looked at me
with large questioning eyes, wanting to be contradicted;

and the waves rattling uncertainly over the shoals at Entra,
the gulls are quiet again and it's only the dog

sleeping, half-blind like me, whimpering in his sleep.
He's deep in his dream, his warm furry

animal dream, I won't be able to follow him
into his dream and there's nothing but water

and waves rattling uncertainly over the shoals,
and, you understand, this poem might

continue indefinitely, and the same stones,
the same wise round stones that get older than we do,

would be rattled by the same wave in the same wind,
and I'm an eye just an eye seeing.

Shutting an eye can be just as difficult
as shutting an ear, believe it or not.

When a cloud comes between the sun and the northwest rose
window
of Chartres Cathedral, the famous northwest rose window,

silent storms of color surge through the glass.

Lines for the Prince of Venosa

≪*Translated by Yvonne Sandstroem*≫

We leave Robinson here

he was nothing but a character in an adventure story
that everyone's read before.

In November 1971 it was windy (as usual)
a terrible storm, the planes couldn't land.

I sat up until late
with some people in Gothenburg

and understood they didn't understand me (as usual),
fetching up in Lund the next afternoon—

I almost said Holy Lund,
for the wind suddenly stopped blowing.

Professor Ehrenswärd was sitting
behind a very small desk.

During our conversation he kept sucking a milk carton
as if it were a mother's nipple

and he told me about the world of the future,
about·the sailing ships, the hordes of cyclists

going out to the fields at dawn,
the charcoal kilns, the little inns

along the rained-out roads, the sects,
the trains of flagellants, seafarers on a long voyage

to America, the madrigal singing and the reed flutes
in the wide sweep of gardens in April,

proletarians of the plow tilling the soil,
and high up, floating slowly

on the moonlit side of the clouds, the voyagers
in their hot-air balloons.

Yes

beauty is the only thing that lasts.

And I thought of the stones, the stones pure and simple,

because they live so slowly

that they don't even discover our existence.

(Certain quartzes, Caillois tells us,
contain some trapped water
older than all the seas in our world
and it swishes around in the stone's darkness
like a very small, very clean sea.)

Yes

beauty is the only thing that lasts.

It doesn't matter a damn how you misuse your life
you'll still find a way home to yourself

although naturally it isn't the home
you left, faraway.

Mahler and Bruckner wrote enormous slow symphonies
to convince us that death isn't so bad after all;

like the Swedes in the nineteen-seventies
they lived in a technologically advanced monarchy

which no longer believed in itself,
where the postal system already functioned irregularly.

Mahler and Bruckner is a congenial firm;
the immensely slow adagio which closes

Mahler's Ninth Symphony ought to get an award
just like penicillin or polio vaccine.

Together with Mahler and Bruckner,
both of them wearing soulful little eyeglass frames,

stubbornly swaddled in the lap robes against the evening chill,
I went by jeep to an unusually nice place,

the monastery of St. Catherine in the Sinai desert,
an unreal place between red mountains

with admittedly minor parking problems.

Together we viewed the Codex Sinaicus,
the first handwritten manuscript in a Slavic tongue,

demonstrating that Bishop Cyrillus of Ohrid
wasn't so stupid after all

the way those Byzantine louts had always claimed.

And then the guide insisted on showing us the ossuary.
Mahler with Guide Bleu and Bruckner with a cigar

were amazed that the bones of bishops were always kept together
while all other bones are sorted according to kind

as in wholesales Whitman,

"Wrists, and wrist-joints, hand, palm, knuckles, thumb, forefinger,
   finger-joints, finger-nails"

neatly as in a spare parts warehouse
every damn finger joint there was in St. Catherine's

nicely sorted and logged by those Bedouins
who were slaves in the monastery during the early Middle Ages.

It's just like at home in the Cathedral of St. Stephen,
Mahler said, as we came out, putting on his sunglasses,

(the light in the Sinai is nothing to fool with)

(a kind of intense primaeval light over naked mountains
and a man riding becomes immense,
in his dark cloak, a single man
can fill a square mile with solemn presence).

It's because the bishops have to *pull themselves together*
first on the Last Day, Bruckner said,

they must *get on their legs* quickly to take command,
Mahler suggested, like some kind of reserve lieutenants,

"I beat and pound for the dead," said Mahler,
"I blow through my embouchures my loudest and gayest for them."

Yes.

The wind stopped blowing over Holy Lund
and the guardrails on the turnpike were down for long stretches

as if a bad child had been playing with them.
An express train took me to Karlstad

where an old Lapp woman and a hearty football player
were going to read from their memoirs and I from mine.

(When the last decade was still young
Jack Kerouac went first class across the Atlantic.
In the dining room, the second day, he met
a little psychiatrist in gold-frame glasses and silver tie
who wanted to unravel his neuroses.
"Neuroses," Kerouac said, "inhibitions!"
"OK, now we'll see who's inhibited, you or me,
I'll count to three and then we'll drop our pants.")

The acoustics reminded me of the Sture Bath
and the next day the press opined that people from Värmland
generally are better writers
and that Gustafsson, above all, is unnecessarily *learned*

and in the midst of the confusion I saw, in the second row,

the beautiful young Donna Maria d'Avalos
with her red-gold hair, her wonderful lips,
her hairnet worked with pearls, oh ye gods!

Afterward I found her in the bar of the City Hotel
talking to a communist professor
and squabbling with a liberal councilman
at the next table. This gave me my chance.

Donna Maria, I said,
and she presented me with her prettiest smile.

And your husband, the Prince . . .

(I bit my tongue because I remembered a thing or two.)

The Prince, oh yes, the Prince, she answered impassively,

Yes he writes the most beautiful masses and madrigals . . .

Yes

beauty is the only thing that lasts

Mahler and Bruckner. Delicatessen.

A very small sea, completely dark,
trapped in age-old quartz.
Water that's never been in touch with water.
Wet before any dew had fallen
over the sterile desert mountains of our planet.

I came home one night around nine.
New snow had fallen. Already by the fence

my dog nipped my trouser cuffs, jumping about
in the snow. It's nice to feel loved.

Sestina on a Successful Volley

≪*Translated by Yvonne Sandstroem*≫

There was a time when every hour was whole
like the tennis ball that hangs for some
hundredth of a second, poised and waiting
above the net. Not "just" gone by, not "soon"
but some third thing, which is all we see.
The other is a hope for or a time

that's past, but not my own: another's time.
The dry thunk once again will make you whole.
Such are the only real things we see.
Hope and remembrance fill what seems to some
a largely random consciousness; we soon
see him standing, the next ball awaiting.

But who's the one standing beside him, waiting?
All time is eaten up by thoughts of time
that's past, or something that will happen soon.
Hope, and remembrance for the rest. The whole
man is the one no longer seeing some
other ball in that which he can see.

Those events we actually see
unexpectedly prove featureless. Waiting,
past years and late princes seem like some
frozen forms that live in frozen time.
With names we make the broken vessel whole,
carried with care to a well which soon

seems deep and full of mighty voices. Soon
a lonesome echo's left: and you can see
the surface of the water, light and whole.
Far down deep it lies so still and waiting.
It can't be reached. And it is you. Your time
is brief. A single stone suffices. And some

single surface breaks: transformed into some
thousand fragments whose reflections soon
flicker on the stone: and they are time.
The only time we understand. We see
in fragments. In frozen poses we stand waiting.
The dry thunk once again will make you whole.

We're living in some nameless world. We see.
We die as soon as we remember: waiting.
There was a time when every hour was whole.

GUNNAR HARDING

Gunnar Harding (b. 1940) is a poet of journeys and transformations. In eight volumes of poems he has, since 1967, given readers numerous maps and travel records from a continuum of physical (geographical, historical) and metaphysical as well as psychological realms. He has done so without succumbing to the temptations of megalomania or pontifical owlishness that so often, to some degree, disfigure oeuvres of similar scope and ambition.

In his late teens Harding played in several Swedish Dixieland Jazz Revival bands—"more enthusiastic than successful," he says—while studying to become a painter. During military service with the Royal Norrland Dragoons he decided to become a pacifist and poet. His apprenticeship in jazz and in the visual arts served him well from the start. His poems are characterized by a consistently lively balance and tension between vividly visual information and the seemingly effortless musical structure that contains and carries the information.

Harding has also had a distinguished career as editor of a poetry magazine with wide circulation and as translator and anthologist of world poetry in the modernist tradition: his credits include Apollinaire, Cendrars, Khlebnikov, Mayakovsky, Ginsberg, Olson, to name a few.

Without making concessions to fashionable (and therefore, by definition, false) occultism, Harding has become the one poet of his generation deserving the attributes "magical" and "alchemical." It is no accident that his recent works reflect a continuing involvement with the ideas and writing of C. G. Jung.

A. H.

Owl

≪Translated by Gordon Brotherston and Gunnar Harding≫

9 p.m.
two round eyes are switched on
        in the oak. A dull creaking sound
    and the tree is transformed into an owl
with feathers of rough bark, with claws
    of earthy roots. She breaks loose
        a flying tree-trunk, heavy wing-beats
            low over the ground.

    Eyes that see
        how the darkness lives, how the stones light up
and birch weevils glow in the trees, huge illuminated cities
    in the bilberry patch while the moss burns like phosphorus.
        A cold blast of oxygen
    hits the wood anemones. They burn together
till they burst from the terrifying black heat
    explode
        into burning color.

    She carries inside her the world
as it was
        before the stars began to drift across the sky.
        The thoughts of the dead
live in her. Little by little
                she sees the world transformed
            into the world
        inside her.

Lasse-Maja in Carlsten Prison

≪Translated by Anselm Hollo≫

Lasse-Maja, nickname of the notorious thief Lars
Molin, acknowledging the fact that he frequently,
and over extended periods of time, operated in
female disguise. In 1813 he was given a life sen-
tence and incarcerated in the fortress of Carlsten.
He received a pardon in 1838 and died at Arboga
in 1845, at an estimated age of 60. Stories about
his exploits became popular reading matter, and
tradition has it that his redeeming social value
consisted in "taking from the rich and giving to
the poor."

Every night
    the water rises again, every night
he is flooded by his own blood
    infusing him with darkness, every night
the rough beard stubble pushes through
the pores of virginal cheeks. Where can you escape
    when all passages lead back into yourself,
lead only farther into the mountain, into grey walls
        grown out of the rocks, grey cliffs
        grown out of the sea, grey stone walls
    grey stone clouds, waves of grey stone.

Every night, the whole bloody island is immersed
in the sea, like a mousetrap, every night
      the convicts crowded together
      too tight in their own stench, no one knows
whose fear it is keeps him awake. Their chains
    hold them together, the chains
        and the sea and the rocks of Bohuslän
          out of which, every day, in the daytime
          they quarry new stone
          for new prison walls.

Hellyes!, there had been times
    when he too had accomplished sea-change
      from man to woman, times
        he sallied forth in gladness
      in a blue gown, trimmed with lace.
    Yes, once he stole
the entire world
    and stuffed it in his mouth
      and swallowed it. Ate up
the entire world
until it started shining bottle-green
      out of both his eyes.

      Ran, as one possessed,
      holding his skirts
    through the forests by Hjälmare
ran through the sloe thickets, noisy with sparrows
    white legs flashing across the stream
      & down into the beds of maids and hired men,
spilling his seed with the silver candlesticks
    under the mattress, then flying away
      through back doors, chimneys, outhouse shitholes.
    See, it was all there inside him: the woods
the stream, the man, the woman, the fire, the excrement.

Stopped, at last
   by a wall, a stone wall
      not permitting metamorphosis
         or only the final one: the turning
      into stone. And imperceptibly
life shades into the fossil,
   into xylography, so gently, though
      one cannot tell
         if those one addresses
           are of the quick, or the dead.

   High up on the walls the rookies in blue
stride back and forth. Lasse-Maja expels
      a long, brown stream from his mouth
the very same mouth even the Vicar wanted to kiss
      once upon a time. Lasse-Maja
         dictates his "Memoirs"
           to the seagulls
      and if their laughter is strident,
           it still is appreciative.

   He found a tree, its crown
      more like a huge green skirt
to climb and crawl under. The dogs found it too
      and him. Sheriff and ruddy peasants
congregated at the foot of the tree
      and slowly he began
         the long descent

Groaning, in chains
   at the bottom of the black prison cart
      gliding away
         down a darkling lane
   the treetops flowing backward
         across his face.

Hellyes!,
the chains, even the chains
he contained, and the stone. Every night
they pull him down into the dark,
and every day
and every night: iron and stone.
Slowly he sinks into himself, into iron and stone
while the world, little by little,
steals back everything else.

The Black Death

≪*Translated by Robin Fulton*≫

Green the beginning, green
and blue. A ship loaded with English cloth
hits the rocks off Bergen. Under the surface
a pale body glides
through dark water, breaks the surface
opens communications
between the light and the depths. On the deck planks
bodies darken in the sun.

Hang some meat
in a tree.
When it blackens
the plague's come.

And the ship with masts already bursting into leaf
continues
through forests and mountains
through days and nights, through
towns and villages, breathings
so hoarse you beg God
they'll stop, rooms
so cold, only the dead can stand it. Slowly
the tracks vanish astern. Slowly
the forest closes again.

The bells fall silent
and the ax-blows among the tree trunks. In the tower
birds sit
bunched tight, black as the blood
under nails. Silent
as the darkness that follows a scream.

Other days with a cold white light, frozen days
    when you can walk on the water. Burbot
        frozen in the ice, bearded faces
upturned eyes staring at us. Out on the ice
            we club their heads, hack
            them free with crowbars. They
    are our ancestors. We eat them. Slowly
they start eating us from inside.

            Deeper down in the dark
        until you're part of it
    until it's part of you. Other
faces there, more grotesque
                    harder to make out.
            If you've never looked in them
            you'll never see the light.
At night they glide into your dreams
        eat up your name
        until you are only a body
through which the dream flows. Thick lips
        round wide-open mouths and eyes
            swim through you, swallow
            all you want to be
        until you are yourself.

They start unloading
    raise big bales of cloth
from the dark. The signs are unambiguous.
        A buzzard
stationary in the air
            burnt into the sky.

        What you first see is
        a little boy with a rake. He
is dressed in blue. After him
        a little girl comes
            in rags. Grey light
        washes over you.

They're digging a pit. They
   toss both children down
and hastily shovel it over. It
     won't save anyone.
You open the door
        and the darkness washes over you.

And the harvesters holding their sickles—
the ground closes round them, the trees
    close round them. In the wet mould
their bones start shining and give their light
      to the grain. Horses stroll free
    with bloody fetlocks
and thistles tangled in their manes, cows
with bells and heavy udders
        farther and farther away.

In the Middle Ages everyone is dead
    but they travel on inside the trees. The summer sky
    is their sail, the bluest sail
      in the world. Wind stirs
    in the oak tops. The air
from their lungs sets the leafy masses in motion.
And the journey continues
    through seas of green leaves
   through waves
of dark earth.

They sit curled up inside the acorns.
   In little birch-bark jugs they have berry wine
     sweetened with honey. They take a draught now and then
   in the course of history
while they watch the nimble badger
     slowly turn into a pile of ash.

And the woman by the sea
  misses her sailors. She
was a cloud over the sea, was there
long before their time
    as all the unborn
      crying for bodies
    to be born in.

She seeks her lovers, her nipples
  stare into the depths. The whole sea
    flows into her
      in heavy currents of blue black water:
    jellyfish with burning hair
  plaice like dotted suns, swimming butterflies
mackerel with blue stripes and silk-white bellies.

    Listless round opal-eyes
  work loose from dumb faces.
  White-gloved hands wave
swim away two by two. We hear only
  the lonely hearts of the starfish beating
            in nocturnal water

With her fingers she tears the silver bellies, the pink innards,
  lets death into everything. Where are her lovers?
        Her songs seek them
      through all the shells on the shore.
    In the song they're still resting
  heavily between her thighs.

  The plague comes in winter
in worn dogskins, snowflakes on its eyebrows. Snow
    whirls in its nostrils. Comes with ice
  for the eyes of men, with snow
for the pot on the fire.

Comes in summer
sneaking back, from another flank
setting a heath in flames. They cough in the smoke.
Comes back
in the smell of gruel and brown teeth
pushes a knee between their thighs
lifts them and throws them
pours into them
a whirl of snow
into their warm bodies.

And the light streams through their houses
in summer. The darkness
in winter.
Burning logs
they tossed at him. The howl
from inside the flames, from the god
who lives in the fire. The silence
from the white god
who is the snow, who covers
the huts   the ploughed acres
covers the fever   covers the mountains
heavy with stone.

And the ship sails through you. Dead hands
hold the helm. On warm days
filled with sun and wild honey
you see the masts among the conifers. The salmon
flee in great leaps
up the mountains, shining bodies
through the spruce forest. You can't
follow them. They're burning dead bodies
on the shore. The smoke twists away,
a swarm of wild bees
from a hollow trunk.

Take away everything
 and are you left with light or darkness? That
  you don't know. You want everything to stay.
In the darkness you see
 light growing. Inside the light
  still more darkness. From the buzzard's eyes
 it's yourself staring
and from the snake's. He writhes
   between the sharp claws.
 In his eyes your own
cold stare glints. The pattern of the branches
matches the pattern
   in your palms.

 The round church walls
are an eggshell round the black crow
eating them from inside
   chipping his beak through them
 emerging
his wings sticky with egg-white and mortar.
The men of the future are already buried there. The trees
    already grow right through them.
 A ship with dead sailors
sails between the trunks.
 They live in you, rise to the surface in you.
You sink toward their darkness.

SANDRO KEY-ÅBERG

Sandro Key-Åberg (b. 1922, in Germany) spent the first five years of his life in Italy, with a family by the name of Gualtieri; the head of that household was a chef. After that, Key-Åberg was shunted from one Swedish foster home to another. He studied philosophy at the University of Uppsala and says that this probably gave him some insight into his own thinking, but he did not have any genuine talent for the "higher art of cracking philosophical nuts."

Key-Åberg's poems of the 1950s deal with a milieu of rural poverty in Sweden, which during that period was being transformed into an effective welfare and high-energy society. The tone of these works is often reminiscent of the earthy and outspoken aspects of Swedish folk poetry. Key-Åberg was influenced by the Finnish-Swedish modernists whose poetry has tended to be more abrasive and less "academic" than that written in Sweden. *Bittergök* (Bitter Cuckoo, 1954) is a typical title from that period.

In 1964 Key-Åberg reached a wide audience and gained popularity with his collection *Bildade människor:* in Swedish this means both "Educated People" and "Created People." These pictographic poems, each in the shape of a human being, were wide-spectrum parodies of linguistic and psychological clichés. Regrettably, they have resisted all attempts at translation.

His success with these poems may have made it difficult for Key-Åberg to regain his own voice; subsequent collections were somewhat uneven. But in 1972 he published the book *På sin höjd* (At Its Peak), which is, indeed, a high point in his work, a darkly humorous study of the myths of the Swedish welfare state.

123

≪*Translated by Lennart Bruce*≫

Dear life please hurry
grind me to crumbles
between the palms of your hands
Shove me into a heap
in your cupped hand
and lift me close to your mouth
Blow me in among the trees
down across all the upturned eyes of life
tracheae and seed leaves
It's so cold closer to the moon
I'm so much in love with the earth

≪*Translated by Lennart Bruce*≫

There's a smell of varnish in the closet
and tears are crawling along the ceiling

I see her small fat hands
roll bread crumbs of pride

Inside the swollen body
the feverish dream is already raging

and on the palm of the hand the mouth blows forth
a pond for thirsty fantasies

The northern Swedish winter in howling pea coat
held together with safety pins of stars

shoves endless marshes across the table
with its gnarled hands

The short knife peels the tenderness from his fingers
where a blind summer crawls

Humiliation preserved in vinegar
creeps over the dead honeybees of his lips

For a moment I ride a knee
toward the glimpse of a heart

A loneliness with knuckles chewed skinless
drags my life over its body

≪Translated by Lennart Bruce≫

The long leagues to the church
he hates the fir tree in his eye
puts his heart in the pantry
to turn sour
bawls out his blundering kids
his throat dry from longing
lathered with Sunday dreams

The old man is fishing through the ice
worn shiny and itchy by silence

Splash and horror
Devil in the sea
the geezer clinks among ice floes
hollers and snorts
sinks boots first

Arms drooping in the silence
weak in the stomach
until she's fought the old man out of her
She sucks her chest full
packs her bag
unties the goat
throws the key in the ice hole
shuffles down the path
kids dangling

Her eyes shiny buttons
hands in her lap before the priest
The kids walk to the workhouse
at sunrise
straight-backed
right into their feverish dreams
the cloth at the store
flapping before their eyes

≪*Translated by Lennart Bruce*≫

He staggers toward the woodshed
planed down by the caresses
stunned by the wild bruise
blood frothing in the gale
The thaw-day
screaming white against bottomless eyes

Blindly he tears her pants
lays bare her subdued pelvis
pulls up her thighs

Hissing, her excitement goes flat
she flings herself away from him
among chips of wood
spits and claws herself free
escaping into the dark
bleeding profusely in the sky of her soul

Snubs the kids into the yard
rattles at the stove
hollers helplessly at her man
whips herself to fury
in the hot heart's thrashing

≪*Translated by Lennart Bruce*≫

Round as a seal cub
and his machinist's fist on his chest
Come let's go to the cranberry woods

It's fun to rock like a boat against the shore
when love flows yellow like rye pollen

Straddling butter-blond thighs
bumblebee-happy in the snapdragon of passion
life's surface is unruffled and yellow whole cream

Embittered as a winter crow
breath of booze against her cheek
Come quick here behind the outhouse

Desperately rocking like a
filthy cart loaded with potatoes

He cracks his dreams between his teeth
longs for the boniest of lovers
his life an umbrella folding

≪*Translated by Lennart Bruce*≫

What a multitude of gleaming heads
Closely packed shiningly polished stone heads
a vast field of snow-white skulls
a shore of baldheaded rocks
when life pulls back
how the bald community murmurs
what yakety-yak
of countless small concussions
their echoes of dry knockings
reverberating throughout the crowd
what great togetherness what stoneliness
of bony nudgings
what anxiousness throughout the rocky crowd
thrusting forward they move
shove and roll against each other
heads that slide over round little
heads they roll and dart
all together such closeness
shimmering marbles of bone
what a hammer of many
and hard collisions
what a headless life
to be a lonely skull
Oh to live skull by skull
harshly packed
with the small rattling spaces
hidden in the sockets
underneath a vast unfathomable space
that frosty and vaporous lobotomy
with its whirls of sparkling terror
they move they push on

down toward the edge
of the water the ocean soaring
look how brilliantly the waves ride
their tall and galloping horses
the sea rushes up arms spread wide
oh the white frothing bride
thundering life gushes forth
over the gleaming
skull-studded shore

≪Translated by Lennart Bruce≫

Have you seen them, all those
whom life turned its back on?
Are you yourself one of them?

They crowd together, those
who live in the world of the turned-away faces,
they all jostle there behind our backs,
right here among us
while our eyes glow for one another.

They live in the communion of backs,
with shoulder blades before their eyes
and at best
the well-groomed back of a head to talk to!

They know the backsides of humans,
as expressive as ever
the well-greased mouths of society.

They have learned the language of shoulder-shrugging,
the significance of the taut back of a neck
and the ramrod-straightened back

and what an almost
unnoticeable pulling in
of the rear end is supposed to mean!

Yes, they know society's backs,
community's heavy and well-fed behinds,
the broad and massive asses
the powerful shoulders,
the round and well-nourished hips!

How familiar down to the smallest detail
democracy's back,
as it turns on them,
thick, fleshy, and tall!

The parliamentary sinews
swell from well-being
and the productive powers seethe
in the protein-laden muscles!

They crowd together and live all of them
here in their backside world.
The backs are the faces they know!

We don't notice them and thus
our eyes can glow freely
between us, their radiance
a cornflower blue.

But we know where they stand!
We hear them tramping behind our backs.
They cling to our heels
as though they were our shadows.

We sense their sharp
and fetid smell,
we hear their breaths!

What a relief; those rare short moments
when we tear loose from them,
get them off our backs!

≪Translated by Lennart Bruce≫

Sure, I see you, old man,
sitting there with your plaid cap
skulking in a corner of the subway car
on your way to Skärmarbrink!

Gray and downtrodden
in your last
torn and senile years
when baldness tightens
and your facial features split and leave.

Sure, we see you,
you and your likes,
as you well forth like vermin
out of your niches and nooks onto society's floor.
Too many of you, far too many!

Don't try to stand out in a crowd,
don't try to look as if you were a somebody!
Get lost, modest and gray
in the social dusk,
unpretentiousness mist,
act as though you didn't exist!

Don't look into young people's eyes,
it only makes them mad!
Keep your eyelids lowered
and your face quiet
like a glass of water
filled to the brim.
We forgive you nothing,
least of all that you're old!

Ask for no reverence
or appreciation for your gray hairs!
Worship youth,
the future is theirs
or revere us,
the happy middle-aged
bouncing forth with our
best years under the soles of our feet,
the power is ours!

Don't insist on a position and place
or any special favors
in the social pageant.
You have nothing to offer,
not status, capability
or attractive looks
justifying your pretenses and demands.
You have to be content
with the reduced fare,
with whatever you get!

Step aside, you good-for-nothings,
keep away from us who're on the go,
as we come sailing, falling off
down the oceans of the nations
with the biologic tail wind
blowing our hair from behind!
Right on,
your best foot forward!
We have neither time nor money
for consideration or any vacillation
as we try to keep up
with development's rush.

So keep to yourselves, old people!
You're run over by the welfare machine already
in principle mangled to death!

Step aside, go to hell
get out of here
while there's still time
run all you can
get on your way!

≪*Translated by Lennart Bruce*≫

Look, what huge
and distantly radiant
galaxies, what magnificent and
awesomely pulsing space we speak forth
where the suns work their way
through the surging cosmos of language
with the great engines
of gravitation humming inside!
What immense language-ways
we speak forth,
their expanding light
ejecting itself
into the nebulous and violently
deepening in space!

We talk ourselves
farther and farther away
deeper and deeper into
the vast and
chill-flaming language void.
The concepts unfold,
incalculable stars,
with a mysterious
and phosphorous glow
they shine as petals
from the leviathan space-tree
incessantly growing
higher and higher
through luminous veils!

There on the lively
and humming green earth
stands Eskil with a sore on his lip
and his threadbare auxiliary verbs
on the patch of mud
in front of the stable
and sees the gigantic nebulae
of abstractions drifting beyond grasp
in the unfathomable jet-black
void of language!

Look how speech
like glittering shrapnel
arranges itself
in the magnetically charged
force field of logic
into huge patterns
inviolably held together
in the glimmering ice crystals
of the interstellar cold!

Jettisoned into the
thinned and violently
expanding gaseous masses
of language space
the atoms of experience
and the elementary particles of feeling
soar through the light-years'
sparkle of zero degrees,
freed of reality's
heavy and burdensome mass
and without ever colliding!

The tangibility, Mrs. Johansson,
an earthly concreteness
with her five-inch Caesarean scar
and her umbrella from the thirties,
rushes torn and diffused,
a glittering swarm
through the great and
faintly glowing gas cloud
of the language galaxy!

Look, the world of humans leaves
its stuffiness and commotion
and rises into the growing skies'
awesome system
of data and abstractions.
Look, the enormous
and unceasingly radiant arch
of the human identity numbers,
aflame, frozen and grandiose!

LARS LUNDKVIST

Lars Lundkvist (b. 1928) grew up in northern Sweden, though south of Lapland proper. Visiting relatives who lived farther north, he acquired an early familiarity with Lapp culture, and his engagement with that nomadic way of life and myth dominates his early collections: *Offertrumma* (Sacrificial Drum), 1950; *Njaka*, 1953; *Nåjd*, 1961; *Blå berg och en vit sol* (Blue Mountains and a White Sun), 1964. "Njaka" and "nåjd" are Lapp words, incomprehensible even to a Swedish reader: "njaka" is a term for low, hilly ground, and "nåjd" is the word for shaman.

Formally, Lundkvist's poetry relates more to the international modernist tradition than to the Lapp tradition of oral poetry. His vision of the Lapps is somewhat similar to García Lorca's vision of the Spanish Gypsies, and Lundkvist acknowledges Lorca as one of his masters.

In recent years Lundkvist has left the realm of Lapp motifs and dealt with the problems of Sweden's marginal rural areas—desertion of the land, centralization, and so on. In so doing, he has abandoned much of the magic of his language. As with many other Swedish poets of the 1960s, social concerns have become increasingly important in his poetry, and Christian ideas have replaced shamanistic thinking.

His unique contribution may well be the "Lapp" poems.

≪*Translated by Gunnar Harding and Anselm Hollo*≫

I

Rowanberry time in the Virgin's month:
the crane gone from the bog,
the scuttling spider, asleep.

Frost makes white, cold, whiter.
The eye freezes over, like the bird today,
when the blood makes its way out of my mouth,
    and the taste
of a bitter berry is sweeter than wine.

Same landscape: smoke in the valley,
mountain with reindeer, dogs barking, calls
    across the water.
Same forms of snow and dead things,
    movements in bodies, centuries.

The moon guards its ancient hare-tracks;
crosses, still sown, in tin-thread embroidery,
shall keep a dying man's true sign obscured.

II

Vain rite, unprofitable word. Beaver
    clock: strokes of the tongue,
when love is defiled, words soiled
by cruelty. Rite is conjured against with bile.
    Gangrened corpse, twisted
by pain, a whirling vision across the snow:
    who will sacrifice a wolf, burn it to ashes?

Snow: ash forest! Water: smoking root
    in Karg! To slivers of bone
the sun could be changed. Gray dog,
its jaws ice. And the wooden stick,
worm-stung: lent to me by barren Saiva,
    a spike through my hand.

Power over things, treacherous distances!
Power over wild beasts, thunder, death! Power
    to be betrayed by
temporal eras, to bleed in vain, today!

It is not the third time, nor the seventh time.
My limbs stretch out, erode.

≪*Translated by Gunnar Harding and Anselm Hollo*≫

It was so dark in Sarvan Viste.
Even the dogs longed for the sun.

So they sent the cowherdess, Sirka
to look for the sun.

Sirka hurried eastward. A long way she ran,
down to the sea where the forest ended.

There she saw the sun: it lay in a wooden trough
and could not shine.

Sirka wanted to punch a hole in the trough,
let out the sun. She became a bird.

That bird is now black, and lives, in the winter,
in the fast white water.

≪*Translated by Gunnar Harding and Anselm Hollo*≫

Man across the moor. Looked for his calf,
came to a burning stone:

heaven's stone,
fallen in the ptarmigan's nest.

Lay down there. Night came on,
one star in the North.

Goatherds found his frosty bones,
dug a hole.

Saw spider. Heard curlew.
Ate trout for supper.

≪*Translated by Gunnar Harding and Anselm Hollo*≫

Blue mountains and a white sun.
　　But it isn't certain—
the bird is late.

It has been snowing? Lily
　　is mistaken for crowberry shrub,
the sky is red.

Evil times, says the numeral. Evil times.
　　The steeple turns
slowly. The hunter is blowing his horn.

Then an angel sings! The snow-sparrow
　　leaves a seed in my throat.
With the wisdom of seven tales
　　and the blood of three poor devils—

　　"Rejoice,
　　the corn shall be reaped!"

≪Translated by Gunnar Harding and Anselm Hollo≫

Pasture burnt,
    cow gone dry.
Into the village of famine
there came a man, spread horror,
fear, with sick lips, rotten
gut. Lived in a hole. The dogs
avoided his tracks.

 Took, one night, out of his pocket,
leaves, bones from the grave.
Ground them up, on a stone.
Blew into the wind, shouted:
      "Karka!"

The moor turned green, with the reindeers' bread.

≪*Translated by Gunnar Harding and Anselm Hollo*≫

Lightning in the ground: the hazel hen shrilled:
Take it!
Small man scampered off. Went
fast, over the mountain, into a valley.
There lay the lightning.
Lifted it onto his back, blew his nose
on the snow-crust. Turned around, blind.

Wailing in the Lapp tent. Dug in the backpack,
looked for his lightning. Found a branch,
a crooked one.

≪Translated by Gunnar Harding and Anselm Hollo≫

Something fell down through the smoke-hole.
"From above it is given," said the man.

"Yes," said the wife. "Tobacco and salt,
a freshly killed sheep."

More fell down.
"Fishes and bread. Maybe a thread!"

"Yes," said the wife.

Sat there, blind, stirring the trash.
"Die, die!" cried the horned owl,
predicting wrong.

For it was Noah.

≪*Translated by Gunnar Harding and Anselm Hollo*≫

Once much ice was here. Then lived a man
who was a hunter and had three sons.

When the man died, each son wanted to grieve
the most, to get the man's spear.

The eldest took off his clothes, ran out
into the winter night.

"It is cold, father!" he yelled, froze to death.

The second son heated a stone red,
swallowed it.

"It is hot, father!" he yelled, burned up.

The third son said nothing. Tears fell
from his eyes onto the place where the spear lay.

Grass came up. Now the mountains are green.

Event

≪Translated by Gunnar Harding and Anselm Hollo≫

Once I took the bus from Gryssjön to Brån.
Suddenly there were two children standing in the road,
a boy and a girl. The boy pointed at a birch tree
with a magpie's nest.

When the bus hit them, the children were flung into a ditch
that had buttercups and grass growing in it.
We searched a long time, but found no children.

Then the driver shouted:
"Goddam!"
and ran over to the birch tree.

When he came down, he held three things in his hand:
a ring, a spoon, and a silver locket.
In the locket, there was a photograph of a woman
who had died while giving birth, in 1906, his mother.

Dryad

≪Translated by Lennart Bruce≫

She comes from the woods
A pregnant woman
With the odor of sex
And spilt sperm.

Her dress is blue
And the rings she wears
Sparkle with the sand of the Sahara
And the ice
At Queen Mary Horn
When at night she steps soundlessly
Between sage, thistle,
Daphne and straw.

She sings of suffering
Witchcraft and hate
About the eyes of the lover
And the power of love
But her back is made hollow
By cancer and soot
And nobody understands
Her words.

She is everywhere
A pregnant woman
Reeking of sex
And spilt sperm
She is in the ashes of cows
And charred corpses
In cities and towns
Ravaged by war

Now she walks
Through the ghost town nearby
Among battered scythes
And rust-eaten locks
There she puts thirteen
Little black seeds:
Eleven apostles
And an anarchist.

The Fanatic

≪*Translated by Lennart Bruce*≫

At the age of 22 he had an accident in the woods
and got on welfare.
He then decided to write a poem,
the absolute poem, and chose for a subject: A TREE.

In the village he was known as a recluse
who picked up his food and milk from the grocery
at fixed hours, sometimes a bottle of beer.
Then for a week he didn't show up, he had just
become 87.
They hiked up to his hut in the woods.

On the kitchen table were paper and pencil
and there was a faint smell of soft soap.
Bedroom and living room
were filled with papers from floor to ceiling:

notes on systems of roots and times of blossom,
dry rot and number of pine cones,
about cone scales and polypores, mistletoes and nun moths,
wood eaters, beetles, gallflies and rot
and about pine needles, gnawed and encased.

He himself lay dead in the outhouse under a tumbled
pile of wood, which later was hauled to the mill
for manufacture of masonite and alcohol.

LARS NORÉN

The title of Lars Norén's (b. 1944) first collection, *Syrener, snö* (Lilacs, Snow), 1963, might induce readers to expect the beginning of a poetic career of a romantic-elegiac nature: nothing could be further from the truth. Norén's early books arose out of a severe psychic crisis he experienced after his mother's death, and the poems are close to automatic writing, with visions of revulsion and terror cascading over the pages, abruptly, chaotically. He did not even bother to correct misspellings, grammatical errors, or misprints.

Norén has been a prolific author, publishing a new volume of poetry or prose nearly every year since 1963. During the 1970s he has used fewer baroque and surreal images and has approached a form closer to the journal. His aversion to the "literary," the aestheticizing, the too consciously composed has led him to present his poems as he first wrote them.

There may be some cause for complaint about their haphazard construction, but there is no denying their force. The emotional intensity in Norén's poems allows him to fuse the trivial and the fantastic, the occasional and the global, the private and the cryptic. The sense of a living, and lived, reality is stronger in Norén than in the work of any other Swedish poet in this decade.

Written around
a Joyful Self-Portrait

≪*Translated by Gordon Brotherston and Gunnar Harding*≫

Who am I, whisper the weightless
soldiers bicycling by
delayed by a sunspot back in 1954
Who am I, say the wordless
voices, say I receptively—do we
remember that, Christophori!
    That I don't know
You say:
I am as others are
I am unlike as others are
I am as others are who are like me
Others other than I are like me
All others like me are unalike
Who am I then, Solitaire?
You say!
    Up here I am language
that stands and reads inward
making lips yellow-white, mediating
by rote a stoic mental illness
in the youth of the stones, feeling how
something shatters inside them
joyfully and slowly
like love itself,
    solitary work.
Sometimes a poem floors
me like a blinding ball

What's the use?
You say!
Everything!

When I wake up wordless I know
what language is: Something to talk
with between the days
Like a man dressed
in the raggedest widow's weeds
shrieking with laughter

Nothing more tranquil
than the insurrection going on
only a bit away from me

And when I'm complete
I'm gathered together from language and silence
From both halves,
around me, so that I am remembered.

German Song

≪Translated by Gordon Brotherston and Gunnar Harding≫

Along the Spree, from the sabbath-hand of the houses
the Moses babies are put out to float
and rock darkly and darker
and lonely toward the fire that has struck
roots in the streets. High above in smoke
and sun, on the Reich-eagle bridges, the young
hawk-eyed Germans marry
their faces canceled by sensibility and fever.
They stand in uniforms light as
morning robes. The soul cannot
dissolve the silence of their hands. They
incinerate into listening ashes,
release the sickness from the
    holy oak.

Everything Is Sorted Out

≪*Translated by Gordon Brotherston and Gunnar Harding*≫

Everything is sorted out
Only when I die will the horror begin
But today, six-thirty in the gloaming
I can stand on a cupola
like a high diver and see how
people are laid out tidily down there in the light
Carry down the junk that's left over
Just now I sprayed sperm into my wife
And she liked it
The metastases of coition are keys to the wind
We can ask from the balconies
whether we should go abroad instead
or take out the laundry, change
the sheets in any case, buy new bags
for the vacuum cleaner, write a poem every day
and apologize, make a pen friend
Do some washing tonight, mail the piglets
write to the Internal Revenue about our taxes
Embrace Radio Sweden, watch how the eagles
aim into the toilet, phone
Miss Welfare, benefit of mauve-brown eyes, be yet more
yourself, pay the psychiatrist 500 crowns
Take out a mortgage with the Enskilda Bank, think
kindly of Loka, be nobody till you
are Unanimous, as I said Sit quite
still till mother, Britt Norén, aged 52, begins
to burn in her death dress
till she vanishes over to the nursemaids
on Unter den Linden, where no green caterpillars
tumble into the gigantic upper-class apartments

≪*Translated by Gunnar Harding and W. S. Merwin*≫

Today everything
is earnest and hushed.
As at the death of a queen
when the radio changes from light music
to Mozart or Bach.
I don't know why.
Since she isn't listening.
I can almost see
how people leave
each other, how silence
works in the fading fabrics
and how the solitary
gray wasp gropes its way
into its death sleep
in the wound of the dry mountain tree.

≪*Translated by Gunnar Harding and W. S. Merwin*≫

Grasshoppers with gray wings
under stiff intense gown

The tree weathers in the heat
until people walk naked in it
reading Pascal's opened thoughts

Pain wakes us at dawn
and the flying soil blows through tranquil
churchgoing towns
where the child stands tethered to the cart wheel
like a young Dillinger
anointing itself with its eyes

The horsemen disappear in
the light like thoughts

The thoughts set out like Huns
homeless, conceived in places
no longer there

Thirty Words about Flanders

≪*Translated by Gunnar Harding and W. S. Merwin*≫

In Flanders the horsemen
sit like
stuffed categorical imperatives
with gasmasks, helmets, and spears.
The horses chew
from their nosebags, blink
calmly at the flies.
Then light speaks
with tongues.

≪*Translated by Gunnar Harding and W. S. Merwin*≫

Woodcutters in white summer shirts
With heavy blond heads and bull necks
Woodcutters in the Hölderlin beech-forest
Brothers formed of calm and honesty
Who become carpenters in the evening
And the whole forest resounds with the axes'
ringing of Bohemian crystal.

≪*Translated by Gunnar Harding and Anselm Hollo*≫

In the Imperial War Museum
stands the still innocent cabin boy
sixteen and a half years old
with eyes that burned and ran
his belly protruding a little
His mouth goes on drooling
like the barn swallow's egg
By the side of the ship floats a sheepfold
with three half-dead sheep
soaking wet frightened staring animals
bleating and bleating in the shining waves
He gets up then falls again
remains lying still
while a dark stream of blood
slowly wells forth from below
He kicks up a huge grey-winged grasshopper
far out there in the becalmed grass

On Nelly Sachs

≪*Translated by Gunnar Harding and W. S. Merwin*≫

Toward the end
her eyes grew
younger and younger
as though they had been watching
what can be understood but not said
They weighed almost nothing
and must have been like the rabbit's
breath in winter air after it has been shot

≪*Translated by Gunnar Harding and W. S. Merwin*≫

Listening to the way the barbers in the suburbs
sweep into piles the dark lonely hair
and the four hundred stenographers beat
time to the while-you-work tunes
every morning on the radio; that the last
good-bye begins, the moment
I fall in love; that you will never
be sure, clear through, that you're alive;
that the poems hang around me like empty
twisted faces in Nazi paintings; then to
scratch out my impossible transparency,
as the cats scratch out
massacred sparrows from the radiator
of the long car in the twilight

≪Translated by Gunnar Harding and W. S. Merwin≫

I talk, these days, at such a
manic pitch about my inner world because I'm
right at the point of not believing
it's there anymore, point of having to choose
between inner and outer destruction, between
what at this moment is in violent motion
and at the same time, somewhere else, remains
still and without meaning, an awareness
aware of its impending annihilation
or of an awesome sleep that cannot be slept off,
why don't I stop, I don't because
there is no end, the end
that does not exist penetrates and confirms
everything

≪Translated by Gunnar Harding and W. S. Merwin≫

Black car shining in the wet grass, not far
up the road into the woods—four young
people gone fishing, three men, one woman; she
is nobody, in a tranquil and tragic way:
Little drops of blood trickle, ticking, from
the open mouth of a fish, riveted
to the tip of a fishing rod gleaming through the mist:
They tell of a time to come when the dead
are to be a radiant and glorious memory
in the woods without end, and no one
walking there able to wear out their
clothes or their skin anymore

≪Translated by Gunnar Harding and W. S. Merwin≫

While we were still sitting in the laburnum arbor
outside the cafe where the death like snow
had spread over the entire small family
that I had at that time, the dress
crackled like young grasshoppers, on the girl
who had moved apart or sat quietly before us
and stroked the grass, six feet tall,
in her fragile dress, with her brown eyes
which I am approaching, cautiously, for
she no longer knows who she is
nor looks to me for her secret

≪Translated by Gunnar Harding and W. S. Merwin≫

Maybe this road
leads nowhere but someone
is coming from there

≪Translated by Gunnar Harding and W. S. Merwin≫

Two magical horses stand over me
behind my bed in which I am lying
like a small naked boy with sick lungs
    head on the hard clean pillow
in the spotless room
In the neck of the horse on the right a hypodermic is planted
In my left arm a syringe resembling it
On the bed a small bottle holding warm blood
and hanging in the room a large bottle of blood
    with a rubber hose leading from it
to the dark intelligence in the lower horse's
    powerful neck
and out in the garden sisters of the self are playing
tennis with oval rackets and secrets behind their backs
their mother has become a symbol to them
    of the soul's terrifying sickness

≪*Translated by Gunnar Harding and W. S. Merwin*≫

When I travel back to my
own birth and existence
there is no mother there
and I have to give birth to her

GÖRAN PALM

Göran Palm's (b. 1931) first book of poems, *Hundens besök* (The Dog's Visit), 1961, contained the poetic manifesto, "Megafonen i poesiparken" (The Megaphone in the Poetry Park), an irreverent attack on Sweden's modernists of the 1950s, whose work Palm found too idyllic and ingrown. That piece of humorous and ironic provocation was followed by a number of prose articles in which Palm further attacked the prevailing poetic conventions. "By and large, the culture's experience of horses has become minimal, but out there on the hills and dales of poetry we still see ten horses for every tractor." Palm made a case for poetry that would approach the realities of society and quotidian existence by means of a language that could be understood by as many people as possible.

The long poem "Själens furir" ("The Sergeant": originally, "The 'Furir' of the Soul," *furir* being a Swedish Army designation that bears a close punning resemblance to the word *furie*, i.e., fury) may well be Palm's best demonstration of his theories. In a prose polemic, *As Others See Us*, an important text of recent Swedish radicalism, Palm describes the Western world's exploitation of the Third World from the point of view of the oppressed. This is a basic theme in his poetic work, already indicated by the title of the book in which "The Sergeant" first appeared: *Världen ser dig* (The World Sees You), 1964.

Three years later Palm wrote that "The Sergeant" was produced before he had reached his socialist and internationalist position, and thus the poem was not ideologically consistent. "Had I writ-

171

ten that poem today, I would certainly have interpreted the authoritarian patterns in socialist terms."

Lately, Palm has devoted himself mainly to political journalism, but in 1971 he published *Varför har nätterna inga namn?* (Why Do the Nights Have No Names?), a collection of short poems on the dark, unconscious side of life.

The Sergeant

≪*Translated by Siv Cedering Fox*≫

Newly released juvenile delinquents have parole officers,
I have a sergeant.
Our democracy is built on equality, negotiations,
compromise,
but put your ear to your neighbor's breast
and you will hear something else:
commandos, a rattle of chains, Polish Parliament.
What kind of secret slave driver do you have?
I have a sergeant.
Here are some pictures from his life.

Midsummer at the castle.
The Crown Prince is playing croquet with friends
from the prep school. I watch in the sunlight.
When something goes well for his royal majesty,
a sunny smile spreads across the field.
And the sergeant wakes up.

RUN AND TAKE HIS BALL!
Don't stand there like a sheep, applauding
as he passes the third mallet.
Run and take his ball!

Across the street from the department store,
I buy a hotdog from a man who has red, meaty hands.
Midwinter in Stockholm.
Let me at least eat hotdogs in peace, sergeant . . .
Trucks go by on dull snow tires.

Take the catsup and squirt it
in his face!

—Catsup?
—No thank you!
The people behind me are eager
to get to my place in the line.
Warm steam. Who are they?
drivers? stock boys?

Tell them what you think of their IQ!

Block after block has gone into hibernation.
An Italian walks by with a baby carriage.
There is something warm about the lights
in the winter dark. I get my burned hotdog.

Bite his finger instead!
Such people should be kept in their place.

The Consumers' Union is holding a hearing
at the Civic Center. I listen on the balcony
in order to report to one of the papers.
The hall is full. Carl Albert Anderson has been thanked.
They are waiting for the annual report.

Stand up and add a comment
about the Union's foreign policy!
Make them completely speechless.
Say that you, as a consumer,
are completely against last year's
centralization tendencies!

But I don't really understand what that means . . .

That's right. You have simply ignored
the problems that the future of the world
depends on! Discredit yourself as punishment.

No!

Discredit yourself, I say! Keep on
until everyone knows what a phony you are.

For twenty, perhaps thirty years, he has lived inside me.
That's a long time. How did he get there? I don't know.
How did you get your judge? And you your dictator?
He just started giving orders one day.
When I was seven, I was scared to death of a large dog.
He barely had to jump in order to bite my cap.
I wanted to avoid him, but the sergeant dared me:
You are not yellow, are you? He just wants to play.
And the dog played until my pants had to be mended.
I hated the scouts when I was eleven.
Rally to, rally to, rah rah rah!
And I signed up for summer camp.
And then puberty. Perhaps one should whisper
about puberty. It raged all over my body.
Then there were girls, in my class in the gymnasium,
and something more wonderful than world records
entered my vision. No chaperone and "Moonlight Serenade"!
But he cut into every slow foxtrot, nagging:
"She thinks you stink, keep a distance!"
Only polkas with rosy-cheeked girls
could be concluded undisturbed. As time went by
there was less time for sports and more for literature.
The sergeant: You have failed as sportsman,
in the same way you will fail as poet!
Finally I graduated and was going to take a summer job.
I thought: Anything, but not the Merchant Marine.
He answered: To sea! And that was that.
As the years went by one should stop minding,
become more one's own, as they say. Yes, luckily.

And the pressure eases? I'm afraid not.
What happens is that the sergeant becomes one's own.
One doesn't say daddy, God, teacher
or any other such word, instead "the voice of conscience."
Whatever he does, I have to stand behind it.

I cut myself on the bread knife, it hurts a lot.

Think of the children in the Congo!

A naked girlfriend crawls into my bed.

Cut off your little prick!

A car approaches with incredible speed.

Step out in front of it!

The royal guard marches past the castle.

Get in behind the drum major!

A famous actor passes with his wife.

Ask for her autograph!

Pär Lagerkvist steps out of a cab.

Say that *Barrabas*
is the funniest book you ever read!

I send a check to the Red Cross.

Ten bucks in order to forget the suffering
in the world!

An ancient relative comes to visit
after church. She is dressed in black.

Tell her that you think about her
when you masturbate! She needs
a little cheering.

A bus stops. There is a sign
in the window: Friendly Transportation Week.

Elbow your way to the front of the line
and shake the driver's hand cheerfully!

I stop at Hotel Reisen's back door.

Piss while you study the menu.
Why fight nature?

A group of officers leave the bar.

Remind them that you haven't been in the service
for a long time!

A man with a wooden leg comes toward you
on crutches.

Can you stand seeing someone suffer so?
Offer him one of your good legs!

In order to get out of the traffic for a while,
I enter a stationery store. Sixty cents for John Silvers,
Ten cents for the Express.
The saleslady gives me the Evening News.

Take out your water pistol
and wet all her papers!

But I don't have any water pistol . . .

Then spit!

But my mouth is dry . . .

      Strangle her then! Strangle her with the Evening News.

      But I shouldn't exaggerate.
      Sometimes he is silent for ages.
      Then my life is free and dull.

As a city child I dreamed about the country.
That's where one should live! The gentle greenery of trees
in the soul. So I became an English teacher in the provinces.
There was a strange peacefulness there.
I thought for half an hour and was satisfied.
I wrote a small essay and was satisfied.
I drank a glass of port and fell asleep.
When Khrushchev goes somewhere,
the whole world anticipates his steps.
Even tractors wave little flags.
That's the way I experience the country.
Houses greeted me from the first day on.
Birches took me aside and gossiped about the principal.
In every room and moment, a sure stance against life,
but there was just no life to take a stance against. Sit down.
A secretive sound in the distance? Not even that.
Wherever I went, someone was smiling.
One neither rises nor falls, one just shrinks, that is peace.
But what does this have to do with the sergeant?
Nothing. He never went with me. He stayed in the city
and set out traps in our old apartment.
After barely a year, I returned to civilization,
stumbling on the junk: people on the phone,
bills on the table, noise on the street, relatives
in the hallway, protest in the soul.

      You ran away, you milksop, go back!

My world wasn't silent anymore.

There is a moving stillness in supermarkets
when they aren't crowded.
The grocery carts don't stick to each other, they glide by.
I am gathering food at the Safeway one morning.
Is the sergeant hollering something as usual? He is silent.
Frankfurters, jumbo eggs, milk, tomatoes, cod roe.
The shoppers push their carts slowly, alone in their aisles.
I weigh some onions. No, nothing happens.
I weigh some onions. I move on. And now?
I forgot the bread. He seems to be asleep.
A tall hairdo floats by behind a tower of juice.
I buy the bread. He should be screaming by now?
The check-out-girls tiptoe around, as if on moccasins.
I put my hand in the freezer. Reindeer steak.

Why doesn't anybody gossip in the supermarkets?
My groceries are counted. There is an almost unearthly silence.
I pay. He is not sitting in the cash register.
My wagon is shoved aside. Nobody looks up.
Same blind motion as in the aisles.
I walk out on the street with my Safeway bag.
He'll rush at me now? But only the traffic moves.
People are just walking there. I am one of the ones walking with a bag.
Here we walk around with bags, I think, and there is nothing between us
but the peacefulness of the traffic.
We are inside it, we are the traffic.
At the next street corner, I run into my congenial publisher.
Then it happens again.

> Trip him! He is just a damn capitalist
> who wants to keep you down.

We walk down the main street. It is January
and slippery. He says something kind about my
books. I say something kind about his publications.

Don't pretend, he is just flattering you!
Knock off his fur hat.

He slips, suddenly, and falls.

But help him up! Don't you have a heart
in your body? He is just publishing your
unreadable books out of kindness.

He gets up, but limps, slightly.
—Are you OK?

Don't try to avoid things. Tell him he can have
all of the remaining editions, all in all,
for $800. A good price.

—$800?
—Oh, do you need an advance?
—No thank you, was just thinking.

Don't forget it was your fault that he fell,
he might be injured for life!

—Stop in and see me sometime.
We say good-bye with small, standoffish smiles.

Wake me, sergeant, when I fall asleep . . .
I sometimes walk on an icy tundra knowing
the time will soon come,
the limbs will want only one thing, to freeze.
Don't let me fall asleep inside myself.
Pour buckets of water between my sheets, wake me.
I am not a masochist,
listening to the sergeant is not my burden.
I just want to be present

as long as anything keeps happening, wake me, sergeant.
Someone is walking ahead, someone is walking behind the patrol
or are all of them disappearing in the snowstorm?
The real enemy is neither he
nor the world's deep-frozen wind,
it is that which is silent inside me,
that which cuts everything off,
that which is becoming nameless inside me,
like a snake in the arms of a sleeper.
I know what you can do and undo,
but the slow numbness will soon reach the eyes,
soon only shinbones will walk on the tundra,
shinbones walking alone—that is worse.
Wake that which falls asleep inside me, sergeant,
wake that which falls asleep inside me. . . .

≪*Translated by Siv Cedering Fox*≫

When death frightens, call it "peace,"
When the empty apartment frightens, call it "home."
When the crowd in the street frightens, call it "togetherness."
When global suppression frightens, call it "commerce."
When government of the elite frightens, call it "government of the
people."
When the state frightens, call it "community."
When chaos frightens, call it "freedom."
When force frightens, call it "law."
When the night frightens, call it "day."
Call it Sunday or Monday.
The days change name in the middle of the night, as if the sun
never set
(The sun never sets on a language that lies.)

≪*Translated by Siv Cedering Fox*≫

114

Why don't the nights have any names?
Because half of our life, just half
of our life is not known to us. Not
to any of us.

≪*Translated by Siv Cedering Fox*≫

120

Suddenly we have a daughter in the house.
The night became soft as a fur coat when she came.
Now we are learning how to crawl again.
The whole block answers to the name Mona.

MARGARETA RENBERG

Margareta Renberg (b. 1945) belongs to the generation of poets who first appeared in print during the 1970s. Without engaging in any direct polemic against the preceding generation, many of these poets moved in entirely different directions, often taking up an earlier, modernistic tradition. Renberg can be seen as a post-surrealist author: hers is a highly concentrated surrealism, in which the heat of the content is offset by the coolness of the verbal expression.

To date Renberg has published only one book, *En tatuerad dams memoarer* (A Tattooed Lady's Memoirs), 1974, in addition to work printed in anthologies and magazines. She is also a promising painter, with a style reminiscent of Giorgio de Chirico or Max Ernst. The following statement is from one of her exhibition catalogs:

"If you want to liberate yourself as far as at all possible to be here and now, you first have to liberate yourself from all your accustomed and false preconceptions. As soon as you become accustomed to continuous critical thinking, you will find it difficult to swallow ready-made 'truths'. But then it is not easy to replace the notions you have lost with others that are truer. This applies to your own ideas about yourself, too. Try! At last you'll see your own mirror image lower its eyes and release you.

"Perhaps you think that these are psychopathological ravings: but remember that a picture of three interwoven sinus curves possibly says more about the true nature of three-phase alternating current than a realistic representation of a length of electric wire and a plug ever could say."

183

From Home

≪Translated by Lennart Bruce≫

Your buzzard has returned
with meat in its beak.
Your dove with green leaves.
The water is receding and you
pack your bags.
Early tomorrow
a glove lies
empty as disillusioned
motherhood,
huge like a body and black
in the frost-white grass.
Don't kick it
ungrateful daughter!
Take a detour as you leave
our house!

Drawing

≪Translated by Lennart Bruce≫

Your face is pale
as quicklime.
Don't laugh.

I drew your portrait
in the lime dust
with a straw.
But I didn't spit
didn't piss
didn't shed any tears
on your face.

You're pale
like quicklime.
Don't cry.

The Farewell Letter

≪Translated by Lennart Bruce≫

He wanted the lines
in the palm of her hand
but no part
of its skin.
He wanted the arc
of her eyebrow
but not one
of its hairs.

She tired of longing
to be touched
most decidedly so
when she touched him.
From the airport
she mailed the letter
with the cut pieces of fingernails
dandruff and hair from her brush.

"I don't understand,"
he said.
"I asked for so
little. Almost nothing."

At an Outdoor Café

≪Translated by Lennart Bruce≫

We must have been bitter
that day after the rain
because whatever we said
the words bounced
off the surface of the garden table
and whipped the one who spoke
over the mouth.
"Something strange
is happening here,"
somebody said.
And our smiles
waited like ice-cold
drops in the tree.

Morning Conversation

≪*Translated by Lennart Bruce*≫

"Understand me?
You'll never"
—but emphasize the never,
the tragic nostrils and
a bitter smile,
not becoming to him.
Then we compared nightmares
and a snake farm
is nothing to boast about
at the restaurant
where the brains are served
humanly warm
in their natural juices
in their natural bowl

(Yet another note
on how much love
I haven't paid for.)

Prayer to My Joy

≪Translated by Lennart Bruce≫

Joy, swallow me
without first plucking
my feathers.
Kill me again.
Give birth to me anew.
Sing me a ball of fire
when I weep.
Stamp my passport
out of this circle
of dog heads.

Weekend

≪Translated by Lennart Bruce≫

We compared our treasures
(in accordance with the ritual)
shiny porcelain eyes
the most common
grotesque photos
the dead insects
gathered from windowsills

Nights
I smoked cigarettes
and listened to
the others breathing
(only I didn't take
any sleeping tablets)

Since the moment
I touched the dead man
(I wanted to show them
he wasn't dangerous)
they were afraid of me

Movies

≪*Translated by Lennart Bruce*≫

Thirty-two stills
a second.
The images live and move
through the inertness of our eyes.
The woman so skillfully balancing
on her high heels
her two bird craniums,
hides a gun
and a dead fetus
in her handbag.
The man at the oak desk
has been using
a number of aliases,
one of them he guards a strict secret.
If he forgets it he'll die.
If she gives it away
he'll turn into stone.
But her present name
is no secret.
And her used up name
is nothing but
flakes of ash in the draft of wind.
And now it's you
dear spectator
who must decide
if the light of this scene
may be
a kind of faked darkness.

Things You Can't Talk About . . .

≪Translated by Lennart Bruce≫

Everybody asked him why
he'd painted the picture
of the burning heart.
But: "Be quiet!" he said
"it's a secret."

That's the way it is
with secrets . . .
One morning you're wakened
from the swelling tongue
exploding in your mouth.

One morning you wake
unharmed in the ruins
of a house burned down.

Isaac Newton's Second Wakening

≪Translated by Lennart Bruce≫

The firm fingers of the ribcage
loosen their grip
around the man
who falls down the stairs.
His skin like wet paper.
His heart tumbles down the stairs.
It hits every step.
His heart breaks
at the foot of the stairs.
A seagull flies
under clouds opening up.
A chest
full of apples.
Loaded with acid apples
the ambulances speed through the city.
And the gull high above the street
quiet quiet
between the walls of houses.
Your head is hit
by yet another beating heart.
The pendulum of your violence
swings high
sinks low
swings high and stops
high.

Declaration

≪Translated by Lennart Bruce≫

I claim solidarity with my heart.
I'm not speaking symbolically now.
I'm speaking of the heart literally,
the muscle that pumps the blood
through the veins and arteries
that I also claim solidarity with.

I claim solidarity
with my convoluted brain,
the sex organs, the intestinal villi
and the magic parts of the body;
nails, hair and teeth.

Once I was a great beauty
all dressed in fur with striped sides.
But they put me in an electrolytic bath
in order to tattoo me.
But it's silly to regret
a lost virginity.

My skin is irrevocably tainted.
The only solution is to finish the work
covering the whole body with tattoos.
The only solution is to strangle the tattoo artist
with the cord of his electric needle
and take over the means of production.

ÖSTEN SJÖSTRAND

"When the morning breeze is blowing and the shadows disperse, this is what I often see: the blue-green, shimmering water, and the rock, the warm West Coast granite. The firm rock and the quick water—to those I return. . . . Indeed I experience the water and the rocks as two basic elements within me. My dreams confirm this." Thus Östen Sjöstrand (b. 1925) on the two fundamentals of his poetry. Born by the ocean on the West Coast of Sweden, he spent a great deal of time with an oceanography professor while still a child and was fascinated at an early age by the model of reality provided by the new physics.

Sjöstrand made his first appearance in the 1950s as a Catholic intellectual poet—a rare phenomenon in Sweden. Although he left the Catholic church, Sjöstrand manifests his own kind of mystical religiosity. Modern music is another of his interests; he has written essays on, among others, Scriabin and Ravel. He has also translated a number of opera libretti. At present Sjöstrand is a member of the Swedish Academy and the editor of its journal.

In essays such as "The Necessity of Fantasy" and "Is the Beautiful Out of Date?" Sjöstrand has made a case for the dream as a means of cognition and source of energy, not least for poetry, as well as for the poem's right to be "merely" a poem. In *The Dream Is Not a Façade*, his collection published in 1971, he demonstrates the presence of creation myths in the living psyche: deep down we are connected to the primal oceans. Sjöstrand is utterly convinced that he, investigating his own "inner bedrock," speaks of matters that are of equally primal importance in other people's lives.

Wisdom

≪Translated by Robin Fulton≫

I

Lamenting, in the cave of ambiguous confession, in the secret
darkness apart . . .
Upright, in the regained light of day, close by the olive tree.
(With the
sparkling cells, the playing thoughts, protected by the
shining helmet!)

You saw Her triumphal coach, drawn by white runners, at a court in
Ferrara.
But the olive sprig was broken, for the true Minerva: the wind of
Wisdom,
Hagia Sofia!

II

And where is her life-giving breath and calling now?
In the inquiring thought, in the possible city, at the heart of
perpetually
reborn activity;
where the eight-fold way opens out, in the fragments of created
matter, the
sought genetic code;
in the mutations of the human sea, that inner sea which also heaves
toward
the moon, some degrees warmer: with us—your creators,
O God!

Burning Alphabet

≪*Translated by Robin Fulton*≫

The book is opened, and the earthly letters are split, are broken in
two in SHANTIVANAM The forest of peace, in CHING-TU The
pure earth in a close spirit who was oppressed by Trofonio's
oracle Or: by silence (after the boasting of the chieftain's halls,
the trumpet blasts of the royal palaces) which was oppressed by
silence in an unknown temple's holiest of holies:
I move forward letter by letter

The book is opened. And the earthly letters are sundered, are
broken in two like the hand ax in an unknown enemy hand, the
arrowhead tips and the scrapings in an unknown ally's hand
I move forward letter by letter —

TS'IN-SHÏ HUANG-TI built The Great Wall HUI YUAN lived
there CHU-HI lived inside there CHUANG-TSÏ lived inside
there The serving brother TRA PA lived, worked inside there

PHIDIAS! POLYGNOTOS! ASKLEPIOS! APPIUS CLAUDIUS!
ORIGENES! PALAMAS —

But the garden where the nightingale sang The Great Flood has
inundated: Those who were drawn under the Bell to the water
of madness other waters have shrouded in burning and cold
silence —

but I move forward letter by letter, I put together

HERODOTOS PLUTARKOS DIO CASSIUS ANNA KOMNENA
BARONIUS TILLEMONT DUCANGE—and QUINTILLIANUS
with his antiquated art of education FRONTINUS who knew
how the water
was once led in The Great City—
their syllables, The Chronicle, were torn to pieces by a rushing
heartless
ring nebula, but:
I go on moving forward letter by letter

I go on moving forward letter by letter
through the mouldering masks and wooden gods of a stone age,
through the
corroded metals, through the green TARA the white TARA, I
move forward
letter by letter in a still memory-thronged music of ideas, under
ONE
letter: the Tau-cross, the Cross-gallow, the letter T—

Those who quote rebirth among colonnades, rosette windows,
stupas,
and order the whiplash, they laugh:
those who among imitation source-streams and rivers distribute
lime
and crushed glass, they laugh;
those who spread the new leprosy tablets, they laugh,
those who prescribe the wheel's terror for wakening eyes, who
color
the ironed ripped clothing with blood,
they laugh—

Those who beheld RISHI Those who plunged into the depth of
divinity see it with tears with tears—

In the darkness a cursing crowd draws past, raging and reeling,
    past: the time of polemic is over —

Alone With others On a lurching caique In a train corridor crammed
    with bundles and faith I travel to Tinos, to Lourdes, to Benares:
    with a gathering mind
        I am traveling on rain-wet and dry dusty roads
        to Medina, to Tun Huang, to Mai Chi Shan,
        to the footprints on the holy mountain Sri Pada: am traveling
            inward in the gathering darkness, to an altar of the galactic
            clusters where the words whiten but thoughts meet: to
            Czestochowa, Kirk Bizze, Dura Europos, to the shaft with
            the unburned bodies
        and the empty, holy grave in the midst of matter — emptiness?
        No, still an element in the sought equation.

I shall continue, I go on moving forward letter by letter, although
    the Book is opened, the earthly letters are sundered —

EIDOLON I read: An image of man: the Shadow's serpent:
A butterfly, a bird —

See, with an elephant head, with a body like an armadillo rises
    MAKARA MAKARA MAKABRA KADABRA — Wisdom's shape
    rises PRAJNAPARAMITA —

Sweden is now a Good Friday with Pergolesi's passion music
    streaming out of
        the open windows: the first summers on Ekolsund:
        and the voices that sing: "Oh my people,
        what have I done unto You," POPULE MEUS POPULE MEUS —

The Book is opened. There is written all the good, all the evil in
    life pursued by men.
                    I know: I possess nothing.

But, with a stranger's gaze, with the eyes of a sleepwalker on this unknown planet, I move onward from letter to letter in the sought, the found alphabet: I have won through to syntax: I form my first sentence: I continue . . .

The Very Moment

≪*Translated by Robin Fulton*≫

I

Like a wave washing through the primary rocks themselves
    so She spoke within me,
so Her being called forth the healing
    all-demanding Light:
in the concrete cubes, the human cells,
    the transitory dwelling places!

A violent erupting wind which said No
    to the spirit of thralldom,
to chance, to the predetermined end!

    Anew, thought denied
the prearranged pattern: dominion of the ant-heap,
    dominion of the crystal,
the frozen line's architecture and the Ages of Man!

All at once the tilted pavement was leveled,
    there was security—like the thoroughfare
six miles high. Yet, still higher: I stepped over
    the decisive threshold—
    to infinity, the new age.

She spoke, formed of the same elements as I.

II

A conductive matter? An unbroken will, from uranium to
    lead, in heat and acid?

—For the rapacious, the greedy of gain: roof beams that will break,
the stone
thrown against themselves . . . For all the unselfish, unafraid
spirits (on the
sea that She beheld):
The Sign which prompted them forward!

Oh,
almost free from her veil
She curved the cupola over Byzantium.
She turned to the top of the hill of purification
the bold visionary's eyes. It gave him courage, in the light bursting
out,
in the rush of the moment, to see: not the network of compulsion,
fate's
linked steps,
but harnessed energy. His hearing trembled
to the Song . . .

Turned
to the cinema screen, the TV screen, the comic strip,
the American nude, the conditioned
public is disturbed by the contradictory speech,
by the unreduced, unreproduced
Voice!

The lament of the flesh on the lit streets, the free,
contaminated fields!

—Does She descend, in the shape of a beast of prey,
with a remote-controlled robot?
Does she accompany heart and thought
through the unknown radiation belts,
the wandering magnetic fields? The common effort to launch
a new space-probe?

Now as before: with the instruments
    of devastation
and the all-shaping parturition!

III

The ashes floating above the ciphers and the workrooms
    were all at once dispersed,
the planetary distances were lessened . . .

The newly opened leaves could not hide the arms
    which by the multistory blocks in the mist
were raised to the sun . . .

The rough stem could not check the wind
    which by the dawning suburban square
suddenly assumed skin, and muscles, and eyes!

The light's breath! The liberated heavy thud in rail-joints
    and steamer hulls.
The new wells, the arithmetic of bread!

Inside the eyes' lenses
                the lightning suddenly struck root.
    The stone stood not against the Spirit.
The eye was no camera
                (simply) . . .

IV

Yes, the headlines rained. The human sea heaved,
    swelled. The chasms widened between
contradictions, plunged more abruptly than for Job. But,

a four-limbed fish broke out of the cavern side,
    the medieval wall—I saw it
(in a red-shift spectrum).

A four-footed world sought hold for its hands,
    examined, measured by the eye—
I saw it (in a blue-shift spectrum).

I saw
        on this side of the coal and the oil and the tar
    a place of the skull
become a genesis point. In the four fields
    on a limestone sarcophagus:
the heavy eyebrows, and then the human brows!

In the pause—between two pulse beats, two bursts of fire—
    I read (as on leaflets
announcing peace): "Before the depths I was,
    before the dust condensed,
the least elements were split. Thre I was
    in the thinking matter
as the Gate
        to the forces of creation . . ."

It was the voice of Wisdom—She, who raised her cry
    at the entry to the city—
where the waters, the dreaded, clarifying, suddenly,
    in that single enduring moment,
burst into light. Out of us—millions, milliards—
    out of our being's
intergalactic heart! . . . God, ever closer to You.

            V

Like a wave washing through the primary rock and the firmament,
    so She spoke within me,
so Her being called forth the healing, indivisible
    Claim, the indivisible Promise.

Here!
among time's weeds, oblivion's slag and slaughterhouses:
    the shaping will, and the Leap!
And the power to say no. To the clamorous sleep,
    the facades and the labyrinth,
the lawbook of established disorder. No,
    not the equilibrium of death. Or
the dissection of an overcoat. Or: the flight
    of the chameleons, of the slaves, of the emperors
to the seemingly uniform wall—the disguises
    of self-denial and self-adoration . . .

    But the calling
            to follow, to be faithful to.

    She brushed aside
the prehistoric walls, the commonplace obstacles—

    She led me over
the decisive threshold—to the Poem,
    thermonuclear energy,
the liberated Common Spirit. And I knew
    what the great numbers
hold back, what the measuring minds,
    the comparing thought,
not alone achieve.

After degradation (spilt water)
    the new trust.

The Hidden Music

≪Translated by Robin Fulton≫

"Be cheerful, sir, our revels now are ended."

I

Time of the earth-crust.
Time of the galactic star-clusters.
Time of the wagtail.

Once:
an oceanic movement,
a wave to imitate.

Now: the countless
sunlit dust-specks trembling
in each opening window.

In the rose-window of equations.
In the cathedral of mathematics—

a world which still lives
with us, with the mind and senses of man,
with men who measure—
who discover new, fleeing
star-clusters beyond the horizon
and reach out toward echoes

of voices, beyond the sea ice and the ground frost
and sleepless nights
in cities, where the groundwater dries—

voices we loved, love . . .

Patiently, tirelessly,
we seek to free matter itself,
the frozen spirit.

Some time: time of man . . .

II

While shining night clouds,
dark nebulae, draw past,
I listen — not

to the sunk cathedral's bells
which fall silent
with the distant ocean.

I hear a pulsing universe
inside my closed eyelids.

A Day of Clarification

≪Translated by Robin Fulton≫

The long shore, where the stones shine,
in autumn. Where the clear seawater
in the fjord dazzles with its width, in autum.

The troll of the flat desolation is driven away
one day. And one day the Disturber from the depths does not
what the eyes hold fast to.   contradict

One day the eyes see also beyond the stones
and the water. In the City Park the leaves swirl
in a wind I suddenly no longer dread.

Each Particle
Has the Whole Universe
for Its Field of Activity

≪Translated by Robin Fulton≫

On a bitter country lane, among feverous fish,
the endless retinue of cripples and cattle,
he abandons the circle for the orb and for the Sphere.

On a bitter country lane, where the words have become
syllables of dust, phrases
of frost and the scorching sun,

the aching sleepless thoughts have been touched
by the incomprehensible depths: as by galaxies
heard, never seen. Freshwater—

Freshwater, Plowland, Implements, Schools—
Although the list still sounds like a rattle,
a wooden clapper—his eyes still only see

the Destroyer's white mules, a down-turned setsquare;
the broken terrestrial chain, of friends
and habits, is healed. He is reunited

with the millions of years and the country lane, with the Cosmos.
He will soon, beyond the feverous fish,
see anew: the Irrigation System,

the Housebuilding Projects, the original sign
of the Living Fish: he has already said yes.

GÖRAN SONNEVI

Although he is far from being an agitator and hardly ever makes public pronouncements outside his poetry, Göran Sonnevi (b. 1939) is Sweden's leading politically committed poet. He is also one of his generation's most popular public readers of his own poems, although his delivery is quiet and diffident. After contemplating a career as a chemical engineer, Sonnevi experienced a change of heart at the age of eighteen, started writing poems, and went to college to study literature and philosophy. A few years later he translated Ezra Pound's "Pisan Cantos" into Swedish. Scientific literature is an integral part of his reading, and this is reflected in his poetry, in the content and the clarity of diction.

Sonnevi first made his mark—which also heralded a period of politically committed poetry in Sweden—with the publication of his poem "On the War in Vietnam" in a literary magazine. The poem caused extensive polemics in the daily press on the subject of a poet's, any poet's, ability to influence political events. "The poem about oppression has to originate not in our involvement but in our disengagement. I believe that it is possible to turn even that disengagement into a strength. We cannot empathize, but we can stand outside and refuse to comprehend those arguments advanced by the powers of oppression—about forces in motion, historical causes, protective strategies and so forth," one critic wrote.

"On the War in Vietnam" was, essentially, a statement of the poet's moral indignation over the war waged by the United States. Sonnevi went on to develop that stance in a socialist direction. This culminated in his book *The Impossible*, 1975, a collection of more than 400 pages, longer than the entire body of his poems until that date.

Sonnevi's work is based on the conviction that it is possible to change the world. He told an interviewer: "Criticism and raising of awareness are necessary to ensure that this change will not be blind, but conscious. Writing poems is the mode of expression that gives me the greatest possibility to make myself really clear."

Zero

≪*Translated by Robert Bly*≫

There's more light when I fall asleep than when I wake
That means:
my private death, but
also — the world's
economy spinning faster and faster
life and death
going around wildly
There's more light when I fall asleep
I'm asleep now
No one can wake me
Facing the Alfa Laval factory a smaller plant:
once the Clio Works, now
The Scandinavian Gear Factory, Inc.
I feel the wheels
going faster, lights flashing on and off
once a minute, once a second
I'm alive in microseconds
I'm nearly dead
The bones in my skull
have stopped expanding
I'm shrinking
I'm going around so fast
I look motionless and now
zero!
The dark circle is opening disappears
The private agony is opening
all of us here
are vanishing   Pain
is opening

We don't live anymore
We start things
Start to open wake up
The bed, the house keels over, shaking, rocking,
The sun goes on burning
through every window in the house
it rolls in
I've got it in my skullbones, what is
waking up, what
is sleeping, wants to get out. It is
the bomb
that I've got in my skull that wants
to get out
The private bomb   Our only defense
against FEAR OF CHINA   You've
got it   You're afraid

≪Translated by Robert Bly≫

You are a murderer!
Your white
rigid TV face
breathes
We sit quietly, motionless
We get ready
for the murder
You grow larger, take
our shape, underneath
the skin, cut off
from our bodies
What community
can we make
that could ever
save us from you?
You are a human being
We are
not human beings
We boil away gradually in the white
air here in the room
Your mouth
opens, makes airshapes
that get rigid
and then slip inside us—
long, falling bodies
with mouth two eyes, white,
looking from the screen, out into
another space, still whiter

Through the Open Door

≪Translated by Robert Bly≫

Then a small and pregnant cat walked
into the room, looked
at me, went into the kitchen and
then out again
what if she intends to have her kittens here!
In her womb
a ball of sleeping catfetuses
blind, with matted
licked fur   She's looking for
some place she can have them
where no one will
take the young ones and flush them down
the toilet
She isn't afraid
and she's used to human beings
There's no place here
No security
There sits a human's thinking head
trying to get things unraveled
The head there
only a tiny part of it is working
The head is
almost endlessly immense
compared to that part
a ball of sleeping kittens!
Now a picture appears
of a very small child
who for the first time
lifts his heavy head from the floor
and looks out through the door

The Double Movement

≪*Translated by Robert Bly*≫

There's only a short time left, we will die soon
my body
starts to dissolve, the cells controlled
by unknown forces in the genes
Take a key and turn it!
It jams in the lock
Maybe
I could take off my skin, stretch it
between fall branches
like new, fantastic leaves, it also
would wither, but remain hanging
like bats
the clear fall evening in the old city of Stockholm
I heard the sound of the bats
without getting it
They are new messages, meaning
there is a hellishly short time
If we don't get it we will surely die
Give me
the keys to my body-functions
then I'll
open all the locks at once, be destroyed
I want that!
Inside my head there is a double movement going on
an upward stream,
color light red, brilliant
The heart pumps
new blood to all the cells   They break
down, are destroyed

The walls between them disappear
The body is
dissolved, pure energy
The powerful force field between us
holds it together

A Ball

≪Translated by Robert Bly≫

One morning after heavy
dew at night
angleworms wound together
in a big ball
lay in the cellar well
we couldn't figure out what
it was at first
then we got it
We stood looking at it
a long time
It didn't move much
The ball clung together
blindly, as if the pattern
were biological
It provided protection
briefly from dryness
When, later, I started
to lift it, it began
breaking up
The temporary structure
fell apart, and the ball
lay flat and crawling on the spade
We watched it
without knowing what was going on
I put it down
on naked earth, carefully and in the shade
so that the worms
wouldn't go and die
later in the day

On the War in Vietnam

≪Translated by Robert Bly≫

Beyond the TV set, outdoors
the light changed. The dark slowly became
grayish, and the trees stood out
black in the clear pale light
of the new snow. Now it is morning,
everything snowed in. I go out
to clear a path
On the radio I hear the US
has published a white paper
on the war in VIETNAM
accusing North Vietnam
of aggression. On TV
last night,
we saw a film clip taken with
the Vietcong; we could hear
the muffled fluttering
of helicopter propellers
from the ground, from the side being
shot at. In another film
a few weeks ago
CBS interviewed American
helicopter pilots. One of them
described the release he got
when he finnally got a shot at
a "VC"; the rockets
threw the VC about nine feet
straight ahead. There's no doubt
we'll have more snow today,
my neighbor says, dressed black
on the way to work. He embalms

and is nightwatchman
at an insane asylum. The place where I live—Lund
and outskirts—is becoming a whiter
and whiter paper, the sun rises and shines
burning and cold over the vast pages.
The dead are numbers, they lie down, whirl
like crystals in the wind over fields. Up till now
they figure 2 million have died in Vietnam.
Here hardly anyone dies
except for personal reasons. The Swedish
economy doesn't kill
many, at least
not here at home. No one
makes war on us to protect
his interests. We don't
get burned with napalm
for the good of a feudal freedom.
In the 15th and 16th centuries no napalm.
Toward noon here the sun gets rather high.
Soon it will be March 1965.
Every day more
and more dead in America's repulsive war.
There are snowflakes on the photograph
of President Johnson
taken during the last series of bombing raids
on North Vietnam—he is climbing in
or maybe out of a car—more
and more flakes fall on the white pages.
More dead, more self-righteous defenses,
until everything is snowed under again
during the night that finally
alters the light outside the window.

Will You Come in Here and Get Your Cap On!

≪Translated by Robert Bly≫

Why do I need a cap?
the only place I'm freezing
is my head!
Mama, come quick,
help me! My back
is freezing too, Mama,
burning up!
Throw water on,
then it will burn more!
Then you won't freeze anymore.

Why do I have to come in?
The house is freezing too.
Throw water
on it, then it will burn up!
You are freezing too, Mama.
You're white all
over, and not burning. Listen,
Mama, you take
my cap.
Then you won't freeze anymore.

≪Translated by Robert Bly≫

You shouted to me and said
I'm bleeding,
hurrying! I'm bleeding!

Will the baby come?
Keep still now don't move

◈

You're not bleeding anymore now
Can't it
still be all right?

◈

From the blue-checked cloth in front of me
I blow away many
tiny dried flower parts
that are exactly like magnified sperm

◈

Darling
you haven't bled
since yesterday

◈

A knife edge is lying now
against the thin membranes
before life
Will it
go through?

◈

There won't be any baby this time

◈

I could hear you through the door ask:
Can you tell
if it would have been a girl or a boy?

◈

I sat by you and watched your pulse
slowly get weaker
You got a transfusion
The bottled blood was too cold
I was afraid
that you would die

◈

I looked at you thinking:
You are empty now
Inside you there is a hollow place
where you are in grief
where the dead child used to be

◈

You tell me that worst of all was the sound
You remember
how it ran out
with a slurp

◈

The dead child is alive now
as a part of my body
and as a part of your body

It cannot die

The Island of Koster, 1973

≪*Translated by Robert Bly*≫

A month ago today
we came to the island
late spring, dark trees at night
against a light-filled sky
We met human
beings, penetrated slowly into
the island
A storm came, tore away
leaves and twigs
from trees   Leaves facing west
later burnt
by salt   An island
we know nothing about at all
is at the start
mythic   Each day
is a continual penetration
into some unknown
materia, layers of earth
with mussel shells, old
oyster shells, the ground
black   The sea that surrounds the island
still remote, though
we see it, entering
and leaving the silted
bay where oyster catchers stroll
all day long   During storms
they all lie
flocked, head pointed
the same way, into

the wind   For myself I looked
for a mother image
somewhere in this matter, perhaps also
in the sea   The smaller islands
around the larger island
helped protect me
from that image   I imagined
that seals would soon
give birth out there, the
shortest night
Later we saw seals, beautiful
with changing colors,
but failed to see
any pups
In rock crevices, slanting, hollowed out
passages toward
the underworld deciduous trees
grew there, ash and oak,
up on the mountains
junipers, bent by wind
Beneath the mountain meadows, among
hazelbushes,
orchids, the sort called St. Peter's Keys
Where is the crack
in the mountain, the gentle door
to the underworld
We moved to another house
full of people,
low roofed,
a great calm in the rooms
Now we heard music
Among woven pictures of mothers
shaking their bodies
furiously
The music rose
calmly, turned toward
the feeling rock, the mountain

that moved
Lay on a hard bed
looked at colored yarn in rows
a loom, which wove
more pictures   Lay on my back
as in levitation, in fever
Behind the walls
the greater argument went on
like a jumble
of voices, unfamiliar
that I recognized
Heard the patterns of lies, about
the world fixed once and for all
For the world seen
from some place other
than from inside
the rock, the gentle
rock skin, through
its crack, its
eyes, that open toward
light, there is
only the infinitely elaborate net
of lies
The European Security Conference
went on   It wasn't
its voices I heard, but their
echo, among
the well-read, who have no
power   One voice I imagined
perhaps imagined itself
as the incarnation
of European power
Everything alive is present
on the agenda   The islands lie thrown out
in the sea that is free of objects
The people who live on the islands
lack power,

lack the vision
of what power is, what it is possible
to do   During the summer
the echoes of power spread
over the island, we hear them
call out: "overall plan"
"during this phase of the operation"
bureaucratic
types, bewildered people
on paid vacations, tourists,
readers of books   Lost
in scattered visions
like a cloud of butterflies
On the smaller island
wild strawberries grow, violets,
marsh grass   Saw a woolly mullein
in a little chasm
a Macaon was fluttering
people told me
that its larvae used to hang
on the angelica, which also grew
there   The longtime
inhabitants, mostly
fishermen, and
ex-fishermen, their wives and children, in winter
the isolation, the trawlers
that for months do not come in
because of ice   Visions
in TV, color, voices
which coordinate it all
in a centralized vision, beyond
reality   An eye floats above
the rock, and the gaze waits
until the gentle eye of the rock
cautiously opens
and then burns it out
with dead

light   We moved
to a third house, without running
water, or sink   It didn't take long
to learn all that   The house exposed
to wind from the west
The visions and voices of incoherency
did not fall off   Some people went away
others came   Mothers
vanished, were born
again   I was
their child   When we arrived
the moon floated at night in the south
above islands and ocean   Now the moon floats
over the sea to the west,
over the string of island mountains
there I saw the mountains
of the moon in a tele-
scope, and the sea around them
was dry
The moon is no one's mother
The earth is life's
mother, the sea
is a part of earth
The sea is green, transparent
when it's clean
When water slopped from the industries to the north
doesn't come in
We became afraid to eat the fish
I caught a mackerel
the colors on his back lived
a fantastic shimmering life
then after a few minutes went dead
Wild roses blossomed all over the island
two short weeks
both the deep-pink roses and the variety
almost white   A few days after
the year turned we heard

crickets   The night light
now slowly weakens
and the darkness of the trees seems settled
and firm   In July
some of the voices fall silent
the incoherency increases
Power
undermines it all, reaches out of
everything, pushes up through crevices
from the dead underground
It comes
from all directions
And the body in its attempt to live
sees itself floating
in matter, for an instant
alone
Then it finds itself resting
against another body
resting
upon the underground light and the underground darkness
And the shapes of the rock do not lie
The plants and all the beings
living on the rocks
do not lie in their bodies
And the rock has its eye that sees
The rock under the ocean has
one eye that sees
The rock is formed by wind and water
by the underground
heat, by
the sun's heat,
and by its beings and voices
in the incoherent attempt
to see, which frees
the fundamental energy of matter
in that agonized attempt
to see

But the body's eye
sees, smiles a little
at all of it
Soon we will be gone, all power
will be gone

Now the lark climbs in a lonely small pillar
of song, for an instant she carries
all of it

TOMAS TRANSTRÖMER

Among the books of poetry published in Sweden in 1954, there was a modestly produced and titled volume, *17 Poems*, which marked the beginning of one of the most significant bodies of work produced during the last few decades. Its author was a young student, Tomas Transtömer (b. 1931). The book was so successful that it went into a second printing almost immediately, rare for first collections.

Tranströmer, who is a working psychologist, has since proceeded at his own relatively leisurely pace, producing a slim volume about every four years. *Östersjöar* (Baltics), 1974, is his seventh and, to date, latest book.

Transtömer's poetry combines a mystical world view with language that never lapses into vagueness or mystification. His observations of the natural world are distinguished by extensive knowledge and precise detail: these qualities place him in a Swedish literary tradition going back to the eighteenth-century botanist Linnaeus, which includes authors such as August Strindberg.

Even though Transtömer is an accomplished pianist and deeply involved in music—several of his poems deal with composers and musical experiences—the dominant aspects of his poetry are not musical but visual. His poems are rich in metaphor, yet he does not engage in the surrealist practice of setting the entire poem on fire, letting the images leap like flames from one line to the next: his poems have great stillness, intense wakefulness.

Solitary Swedish Houses

≪*Translated by Robin Fulton*≫

A mix-max of black spruce
and smoking moonbeams.
Here's the croft lying low
and not a sign of life.

Till the morning dew murmurs
and an old man opens
—with a shaky hand—his window
and lets out an owl.

Farther off, the new shack
stands steaming
with the laundry butterfly
fluttering at the corner

in the middle of a dying wood
where the moldering reads
through spectacles of sap
the proceedings of the bark-drillers.

Summer with flaxen-haired rain
or one solitary thundercloud
above a barking dog.
The seed is kicking inside the earth.

Agitated voices, faces
fly in the telephone wires
on stunted rapid wings
across the moorland miles.

The house on an island in the river
brooding on its foundation stones.
Perpetual smoke—they're burning
the forest's secret papers.

The rain wheels in the sky.
The light coils in the river.
Houses on the slope supervise
the waterfall's white oxen.

Autumn with a gang of starlings
holding dawn in check.
The people move stiffly
in the lamplight's theater.

Let them feel without alarm
the camouflaged wings
and God's energy
coiled up in the dark.

Allegro

≪Translated by Robin Fulton≫

I play Haydn after a black day
and feel a simple warmth in my hands.

The keys are willing. Soft hammers strike.
The resonance green, lively and calm.

The music says freedom exists
and someone doesn't pay the emperor tax.

I push down my hands in my Haydnpockets
and imitate a person looking on the world calmly.

I hoist the Haydnflag—it signifies:
"We don't give in. But want peace."

The music is a glass-house on the slope
where the stones fly, the stones roll.

And the stones roll right through
but each pane stays whole.

After Attack

≪Translated by Gunnar Harding and Frederic Will≫

The sick boy.
Locked in a vision
with his tongue stiff as a horn.
He is sitting with his back toward the wheatfield in the picture
The bandage around his jaw makes you think of embalming.
His glasses are thick as a diver's. And everything is without answer
and intense as when the telephone rings in the darkness.
But the picture behind. It is a landscape that gives peace though
                               the wheat is a golden storm.
Sky of blue fire and drifting clouds. Below in the yellow swell
some white shirts are sailing: harvesters—they cast no shadows.

A man is standing far away in the field and seems to look our way.
A broad brim shadows his face.
He seems to be observing the dark figure here in the room, perhaps
                                        to help.
Unnoticed the picture has begun to widen and open behind the sick
brooding boy. It sparkles and hammers. Every straw is lit as if to
                                     wake him!
The other one—in the wheat—makes a sign.

He has come closer.
No one sees it.

Morning Birds

≪*Translated by Gunnar Harding and Frederic Will*≫

I wake my car.
Its windshield is covered with pollen.
I put on my sunglasses
and the song of the birds darkens.

While another man buys a newspaper
in the railroad station
near a large goods wagon
which is entirely red with rust
and stands flickering in the sun.

No emptiness anywhere here.

Straight across the spring warmth a cold corridor
where someone comes hurrying
to say that they are slandering him
all the way up to the Director.

Through a backdoor in the landscape
comes the magpie
black and white, Hel's bird.
And the blackbird moving crisscross
until everything becomes a charcoal drawing,
except for the white sheets on the clothesline:
a Palestrina choir.

No emptiness anywhere here.

Fantastic to feel how my poem grows
while I myself shrink.
It is growing, it takes my place.
It pushes me out of its way.
It throws me out of the nest.
The poem is ready.

Farther In

≪Translated by Robin Fulton≫

On the main road into the city
when the sun is low.
The traffic thickens, crawls.
It is a sluggish dragon glittering.
I am one of the dragon's scales.
Suddenly the red sun is
right in the middle of the windscreen
streaming in.
I am transparent
and writing becomes visible
inside me
words in invisible ink
which appear
when the paper is held over the fire!
I know I must get far away
straight through the city and then
farther until it is time to go out
and walk far in the forest.
Walk in the footprints of the badger.
It gets dark, difficult to see.
In there on the moss lie stones.
One of the stones is precious.
It can change everything
it can make the darkness shine.
It is a switch for the whole country.
Everything depends on it.
Look at it, touch it . . .

The Outpost

≪*Translated by Robin Fulton*≫

I'm ordered out in a heap of stones
like a distinguished corpse from the Iron Age.
The others are back in the tent sleeping
stretched out like spokes in a wheel.

In the tent the stove rules: a big snake
that has swallowed a ball of fire and hisses.
But out in the spring night it is silent
among cold stones that are waiting for day.

Out there in the cold I begin to fly
like a shaman, I fly to her body
with its white marks from her bikini—
we were out in the sun. The moss was warm.

I flit over warm moments
but can't stop for long.
They're whistling me back through space—
I crawl out from the stones. Here and now.

Mission: to be where I am.
Even in that ridiculous, deadly serious
role—I am the place
where creation is working itself out.

Daybreak, the sparse tree trunks
are colored now, the frost-bitten
forest flowers form a silent search party
for someone who has vanished in the dark.

· But to be where I am. And to wait.
I am anxious, stubborn, confused.
Coming events, they're there already!
I know it. They're outside:

a murmuring crowd outside the gate.
They can pass only one by one.
They want in. Why? They're coming
one by one—I am the turnstile.

From "Baltics"

≪*Translated by Samuel Charters*≫

I

It was before the time of radio masts.

My grandfather was a newly licensed pilot. In the almanac he
    wrote down the vessels he piloted —
name, destination, draft:
Examples from 1884:
Steamer Tiger Capt Rowan 16 feet Gefle Furusund
Brig Ocean Capt Andersen 8 feet Sandöfjord Hernösand Furusund
Steamer St Petersburg Capt Libenberg 11 feet Stettin Libau
    Sandhamn

He took them out to the Baltic, through that wonderful labyrinth
    of islands and water.
And those who met on board, and were carried by the same hull
    for a few hours or a few days,
how well did they get to know each other?
Talking in misspelled English, understanding and misunderstanding,
    but very little conscious lying.
How well did they get to know each other?

When it was thick fog: half speed, almost blind. The headland
    coming out of the invisibility with a single stride,
    it was right on them.
Fog horn blasting every other minute. His eyes reading straight
    into the invisible.
(Did he have the labyrinth in his head?)
The minutes went by.
Lands and reefs memorized like hymn verses.
And the feeling of we're-right-here that you have to keep, like
    carrying a pail filled to the brim without spilling a drop.

A glance down into the engine room.
The compound engine, as long lived as a human heart, worked
    with great soft recoiling movements, steel acrobatics, and
    the smells rising from it as from a kitchen.

V

July 30. The channel has become eccentric—today it's teeming
        with jellyfish for the first time in years, they pump
        themselves along with calm consideration, they be-
        long to the same shipping company: AURELIA, they
        drift like flowers after a burial at sea, if you take
        them out of the water all of their shape disappears,
        as when an indescribable truth is lifted up out of
        the silence and formulated into a lifeless mass, yes,
        they're untranslatable, they have to stay in their
        element.

August 2. Something wants to be said, but the words don't agree.
Something that can't be said,
aphasia,
there aren't any words but maybe a style . . .

Sometimes you wake up at night
and quickly throw some words down
on the nearest paper, on the margin of a newspaper
(the words glowing with meaning!)
but in the morning: the same words don't say anything anymore,
    scrawls, misspeakings.
Or fragments of a great nightly style that dragged past?

Music comes to a person, he's a composer, he's played, has a
    career, becomes director of the conservatory.
The trend turns downward, he's blamed by the authorities.
They put up his pupil K—— as chief prosecutor.
He's threatened, demoted, sent away.

After some years the disgrace diminishes, he's rehabilitated.
Then comes the stroke: right-side paralysis and aphasia, can
    grasp only short phrases, says wrong words.
Can, as a result of this, not be touched by advancement or blame.
But the music's still there, he still composes in his own style,
he becomes a medical sensation for the time he has left to live.

He wrote music to texts he no longer understood —
in the same way
we express something with our lives
in that humming chorus of misspeech.

The Death lectures went on for several terms. I was present
together with classmates I didn't know
(who are you?)
— afterward everyone went off on his own, profiles.

I looked at the sky and the earth and straight ahead
and since then I've been writing a long letter to the dead
on a typewriter that doesn't have a ribbon, only a horizon line
so the words beat in vain and nothing stays.

I stand with my hand on the door handle, take the pulse of the
    house.
The walls so full of life
(the children won't dare sleep alone up in the attic — what makes
    me feel safe makes them uneasy.)

August 3. Out there in the damp grass
slithers a greeting from the Middle Ages: Helix pomatia
the subtly gray-gold shining snail with its jaunty house,
introduced by some monks who liked *escargots* — yes, the
    Franciscans were here,
broke stone and burned lime, the island was theirs in 1288, a
    donation from King Magnus
("Thes almes and othres he hath yeven / Thei meteth hym nu he
    entreth hevene.")
the forest fell, the ovens burned, the lime taken by sail

to the building of the monastery . . .
                                    Sister snail
stands almost still in the grass, feelers sucked in
and rolled out, disturbances and hesitation . . .
How like myself in my searching!

The wind that blew so carefully all day —
all the blades of grass are counted on the farthest islets —
has lain down in the middle of the island. The matchstick's
    flame stands straight up.
The sea painting and the forest painting darken together.
Also the foliage of the five-story trees is turning black.
"Every summer is the last." These are empty words
for the creatures at late summer midnight
where the crickets sew on their machines as if possessed
and the Baltic's near
and the lonely water tap stands among the wild rose bushes
like an equestrian statue. The water tastes of iron.

VI

My grandmother's story before it's forgotten: her parents dying
    young,
the father first. When the widow realizes the disease will take
    her too
she walks from house to house, sails from island to island
with her daughter. "Who can take care of Maria?"
A strange house on the other side of the bay takes her in.
They could afford to do it. But the ones that could afford it
    weren't the good ones.
Piety's mask cracks. Maria's childhood ends too soon,
she's an unpaid servant, in perpetual coldness.
Year after year. Perpetually seasick behind the
long oars, the solemn terror
at the table, the expressions, the pike skin crunching

in her mouth: be grateful, be grateful.
                                        She never looked back.
But because of this she could see The New
and seize it.
Break out of the bonds.

I remember her, I used to snuggle against her
and at the moment she died (the moment she passed over?) she
    sent out a thought
so that I, a five-year-old, understood what had happened
a half an hour before they called.

I remember her. But in the next brown photo
someone I don't know —
by the clothes from the middle of the last century.
A man about thirty, the powerful eyebrows,
the face that looks me right in the eye
whispering: "Here I am."
but who "I" am
is something no one remembers anymore. No one.
TB? Isolation?

Once he stopped
on the stony, grass-streaming slope coming up from the sea
and felt the black blindfold in front of his eyes.

Here, behind the thick brush — is it the island's oldest house?
The low, knot-trimmed two-hundred-year-old fisherman's hut,
    with coarse, gray, heavy beams.
And the modern brass padlock has clicked together on all of it,
    shining like the ring in the nose of an old bull
that refuses to get up.
So much crouching wood. And on the roof the ancient tiles that
    collapsed across and on top of each other
(the original pattern erased by the earth's rotation through the
    years)
it reminds me of something . . . I was there . . . wait: it's the old
    Jewish cemetery in Prague

where the dead live closer together than they did in life, the
    stones jammed in, jammed in.
So much encircled love! The tiles with the lichen's letters in an
    unknown language
are the stones in the archipelago people's ghetto cemetery, the
    stones erected and fallen down—

The ramshackle hut shines
with the light of all the people carried by the certain wave, the
    certain wind,
out here to their fates.

Citoyens

≪Translated by Robin Fulton≫

The night after the accident I dreamed of a pockmarked man
who was walking through the alleys singing.
Danton!
Not the other one—Robespierre doesn't take such walks,
Robespierre spends a careful hour each morning on
his toilette. The rest of the day he devotes to The People.
In the paradise of the pamphlets, among the machines of virtue.
Danton—
or the man who wore his mask—
seemed to be standing on stilts.
I saw his face from beneath.
Like the scarred moon, half in light, half in mourning.
I wanted to say something.
A weight in the breast,
the plummet
that makes the clocks go,
the hands turn: year I, year II . . .
A sharp scent like sawdust in the tiger-stalls.
And—as in all dreams—no sun.
But the walls were shining
in the alleys that curved
down to the waiting room, the curved room,
the waiting room where we all . . .

Funchal

≪Translated by Samuel Charters≫

The fish restaurant on the beach, plain, a shack built by
shipwrecked people. Many turn away at the door, but not the
gusts from the sea. A shadow stands in his smoking cabin and fries
two fish according to an old recipe from Atlantis, small explosions
of garlic, oil running over the tomato slices, every bite saying that
the ocean wishes us well, a humming from the deep.

She and I look into each other. Like climbing up the wild blooming
hillsides without feeling the least bit tired. We're on the side of the
animals, we're welcome, we don't get older. But we've experienced
so much together through the years, we remember that, also
moments when we were good for nothing (as when we lined up to
give the flourishing giant blood—he's ordered transfusions) things
that should have separated us if they hadn't bound us closer, and
things we forgot together—but they haven't forgotten us! They've
become dark and light stones, stones in a scattered mosaic. And
now it happens: the fragments fly together, the mosaic comes to
life. It's waiting for us. It's shining from the wall in the hotel
room, a violent and tender design, perhaps a face, we don't have
time to perceive everything as we pull off our clothes . . .

In the evening we go out. The cape's enormous dark blue paw lies
thrown in the sea. We walk in a human whirlpool, pushed around
in a friendly way, soft controls, everyone talking excitedly in that
foreign language. "No man is an island." We become stronger by
them, but also by ourselves, by that thing within us that the other

---

Funchal: the capital of the island Madeira

one can't see. Something that can only meet itself. The deepest
paradox, the garage flower, the ventilator to the good darkness. A
drink that bubbles in empty glasses. A loudspeaker that sends out
silence. A pathway that grows over again after each step. A book
that can be read only in the dark.

The Crosswalk

≪*Translated by Samuel Charters*≫

Icy blast in my eyes and the suns dance
in the tears' kaleidoscope when I cross
the street that's followed me so long, the street
where the Greenland summer shines from the puddles.

Around me swarms all the strength of the street
that remembers nothing and wants nothing.
Deep in the earth under the traffic the unborn
forest waits silently a thousand years.

I have the idea that the street can see me.
Its eyesight is so murky that the sun itself
is becoming a gray string ball in a black space.
But now I'm shining! The street sees me.

From the Winter, 1947

≪*Translated by Samuel Charters*≫

In the daytimes in school the dull swarming fortress.
In the evening I walked home under the signs.
Then came whispering without lips: "Wake up, sleepwalker!"
And all the objects pointed to The Room.

Fifth floor, the room over the yard. The lamp burned
in a circle of terror every night.
I sat without eyelids in the bed, seeing filmstrips
filmstrips of the thoughts of the mentally ill.

As if it were necessary . . .
As if the last of childhood were being broken into pieces
to pass through the grating.
As if it were necessary . . .

I read in a glass book, but saw only the other thing:
the stains that penetrated the wallpaper!
It was the living dead
who wanted to have their portraits painted . . .

Then at dawn came the garbage men
and clattered the garbage cans down there.
The backyard's peaceful gray bells
that rang me to sleep.

The Translators

The Translators

ROBERT BLY lives in Madison, Minnesota, where he was born in 1926. He attended St. Olaf College before receiving the A.B. degree from Harvard University in 1950. Bly is widely known as a poet and does translations from several languages including Swedish, Norwegian, Danish, German, and Spanish. He is founder, editor, and publisher of The Seventies Press (originally The Fifties Press, then The Sixties Press), and he helped form the Minnesota Writers Publishing House.

Among his books of poetry are *Silence in the Snowy Fields* (1962); *The Light around the Body* (1967), which received the National Book Award; *The Teeth Mother Naked at Last* (1970); *Jumping Out of Bed* (1973); *Sleepers Joining Hands* (1973); *Old Man Rubbing His Eyes* (1975); *The Morning Glory* (1975); and *This Body Is Made of Camphor and Gopher Wood* (1977). Bly is editor of *Forty Poems Touching on Recent American History* (1970), *A Poetry Reading against the Vietnam War* (1970), and *The Sea and the Honeycomb* (1971).

His poetry translations include *Twenty Poems of Georg Trakl* (with James Wright, 1961); *Neruda and Vallejo: Selected Poems* (with James Wright and John Knoepfle, 1971); *Lorca and Jiménez: Selected Poems* (1973); *Friends, You Drank Some Darkness: Three Swedish Poets—Martinson, Ekelöf, and Tranströmer* (1975); *The Fish in the Sea Is Not Thirsty: Versions of Kabir* (1975); *Rilke: Ten Sonnets to Orpheus* (1975); and *The Kabir Book: Forty-Four of the Ecstatic Poems of Kabir* (1976). He also translated Selma Lagerlöf's *The Story of Gösta Berling* (1962) and Knut Hamsun's *Hunger* (1967).

GORDON BROTHERSTON lives in Wivenhoe, Essex, and is a professor of literature at the University of Essex. His translations include *Our Word: Guerrilla Poetry from Latin America* (with Ed Dorn, 1968), *Cesar Vallejo: Selected Poems* (with Ed Dorn, 1975), and *Reinaldo Arenas: Hallucinations* (1972). Brotherston translates from Spanish, French, German, Swedish, Maya, and Aztec, and his work has appeared in *Evergreen Review, Seneca Review, Stand, The Review*, and *Sixpack Alcheringa*. He is author of *Manuel Machado: A Reevaluation* (1968), *Latin American Poetry Origins and Presence* (1976), *The Emergence of the Latin American Novel* (1977), and *Image of the New World* (1979).

LENNART BRUCE was born in Stockholm and attended high school and college there. Until 1965 he conducted business activities in Europe, Africa, South America, the Middle East, and the United States. He began writing and translating in California, where he now lives. In 1977 he was awarded the Swedish Academy's prize for translation of poetry. Bruce's poetry includes *Mullioned Window* (1970), *Subpoemas* (1974), and *Exposure* (1975), as well as several other books published in the United States, Sweden, Mexico, and Argentina. His writing has appeared in *American Review, Audit East West, Chelsea, Choice, Massachusetts Review, Milk Quarterly, New Mexico Quarterly, The Nation, Rolling Stone Magazine, Saturday Review, Tennessee Poetry Journal*, and *Unicorn Folio*.

SIV CEDERING FOX has published eight collections of poetry in English, including the prize-winning books *Mother Is, The Juggler*, and *Cup of Cold Water*. She compiled and translated into Swedish an anthology of American Indian poetry, *Det blommande trädet*, and her first children's book, *The Blue Horse*, will be out this spring. Her poetry has been translated into Japanese and Swedish and is included in more than forty anthologies in the United States and other countries. Cedering Fox's translations of primitive and contemporary Swedish poetry have appeared in *Translation, Mundus Artium, Chelsea, Anteaus, Chariton Review, Poetry Now*, and *Alcheringa*. An expanded version of her book of translations, *Two Swedish Poets: Gösta Friberg and Göran Palm*, will be out in 1979, as will *Twenty-Seven Swedish Poems*.

Cedering Fox, who lives in Rye, New York, was born in Sweden and lived there for fifteen years. She is presently translating poetry of Werner Aspenström.

SAMUEL CHARTERS is a writer and translator who has been living in Stockholm since 1971. He has translated the work of a number of Swedish poets, especially the group of writers associated with the Finland-Swedish modernist movement. He is also closely associated with the poet Tomas Tranströmer, and his translation of Tranströmer's *Baltics* appeared in 1975. Charters also translated a selection from the poetry of Edith Södergran, which was published under the title *We Women* in 1977. With his wife, Ann, he recently completed a biographical study of the Soviet poet Vladimir Mayakovsky, which will appear in the spring of 1979. A book about his research into the backgrounds of West African oral poetic narrative will appear early in 1980. Among his own poetry collections are *From a Swedish Notebook*, the elegy *Of Those Who Died*, and the forthcoming *The Swimmer.*

ROBIN FULTON was born in Scotland in 1937 and has published several collections of poetry, including *The Spaces between the Stones* (1971), *The Man with the Surbahar* (1971), *Tree-Lines* (1974), and *Between Flights* (1977). Fulton has translated Swedish poets Lars Gustafsson, Gunnar Harding, Tomas Tranströmer, Östen Sjöstrand, and Werner Aspenström, and received the Artur Lundkvist award for 1977 and the Swedish Academy award for 1978. Fulton published *Contemporary Scottish Poets: Individuals and Contexts* in 1974, edited 37 issues of the quarterly *Lines Review* between 1967 and 1976, and held a Writers' Fellowship at Edinburgh University from 1969 to 1971.

GUNNAR HARDING, born in Sundsvall, Sweden, in 1940, received his B.A. degree in 1967 and began writing cultural articles for newspapers in 1970. From 1971 to 1974 he was director of FIBs lyrikklubb. His poetry collections include *Lokomotivet som frös fast* (The Locomotive Which Froze, 1967), *Den svenska cyklistens sång* (The Song of the Swedish Bicyclist, 1968), *Blommor till James Dean* (Flowers for James Dean, 1969), *Örnen har landat* (The Eagle Has

Landed, 1970), *Guillaume Appollinaires fantastiska liv* (Guillaume Appollinaire's Fantastic Life, 1971), *Skallgång* (The Chase/Search, 1972), and *Ballader* (1975). Harding is known in Sweden for his translations of American underground poetry.

ANSELM HOLLO was born in 1934 in Helsinki, Finland. He has worked as a free-lance translator, writer, book and art critic, producer for the British Broadcasting Corporation, and instructor and lecturer in both translation and writing in England and America. In addition to his many volumes of poetry and numerous magazine publications, Hollo's work has been anthologized in (among others): *Evergreen Review Reader, Shaking the Pumpkin, Open Poetry, America: A Prophecy,* and *Poems Here And Now.* Among his translations are: *Small Change* by François Truffaut; *Some Poems of Paul Klee*; Jean Genet's novel *Querelle*; Brecht's *Jungle of Cities; Selected Poems* by Paavo Haavikko; Georg Büchner's play *Woyzeck*; and *Beautiful Days* by Franz Innerhofer. The most recent and comprehensive collection of his own poetry is *Sojourner Microcosms: New & Selected Poems 1959-1977,* with a foreword by Robert Creeley and an afterword by Edward Dorn, published by Blue Wind Press, Berkeley.

W. S. MERWIN was born in 1927 in New York City and grew up in Union City, New Jersey, and in Scranton, Pennsylvania. He was a tutor in France, Portugal, and Majorca from 1949 to 1951. Probably best known as a poet, Merwin received the Pulitzer Prize in 1972 for *The Carrier of Ladders* (1970). Among his other books of poetry are *A Mask for Janus* (1952), *The Dancing Bears* (1954), *Green with Beasts* (1956), *The Drunk in the Furnace* (1960), *The Moving Target* (1963), *The Lice* (1967), *Writings to an Unfinished Accompaniment* (1973), and *The Compass Flower* (1977). A book of prose, *The Miner's Pale Children,* was published in 1970.

Merwin's translations include *The Poem of the Cid* (1959), *Spanish Ballads* (1960), *The Satires of Persius* (1961), *Lazarillo de Tormes* (1962), *The Song of Roland* (1963), *Selected Translations 1948-1968* (1968), *Transparence of the World* (poems by Jean Follain, 1969), *Osip Mandelstam, Selected Poems* (with Clarence Brown, 1974) *Iphigeneia at Aulis* by Euripides (with George E. Dimock,

Jr., 1977), *Classical Sanskrit Love Poetry* (with J. Moussaieff Masson, 1977), and *Vertical Poetry* (poems by Roberto Juarroz, 1977). Merwin was awarded the Fellowship of the Academy of American Poets in 1974 and received the P.E.N. Translation Prize for 1968.

YVONNE L. SANDSTROEM, born in Västerås, Sweden, in 1933, is an associate professor of English at Southeastern Massachusetts University. From 1952 to 1954 she studied at Lund University, and she received the A.M. and Ph.D. degrees in English from Brown University in 1966 and 1970. She has translated two books of poetry: Lars Gustafsson, *Warm Rooms and Cold* (1975), and Augustin Mannerheim, *rounded with a sleep* (1978). Her translations have appeared in *Scandinavian Studies, First Issue, Mundus Artium*, and *Fiction*. Polaris Theater Company in New York has put on three plays translated by Sandstroem, including: Anderson-Bratt, *The Home*; Werner Aspenström, *The Spiders*; and Lars Gustafsson, *Homage at Night*. Sandstroem is a reviewer of Swedish literature for *Scandinavian Studies* and *World Literature Today*.

THOMAS VANCE and VERA VANCE have published joint translations of Scandinavian poetry in *The Literary Review, Poetry, Granite, First Issue, Conch, Paintbrush*, and the anthology *The Prose Poem*, edited by Michael Benedikt (1976).

Thomas Vance is author of a poetry collection, *Skeleton of Light* (1961), and his individual poems and occasional essays have appeared in *Yale Review, Southern Review, Shenandoah, New Yorker, Atlantic, Poetry, Paintbrush*, and *Parnassus*. He was Fulbright Guest Professor at Tubingen University (1969-70) and has contributed to three scholarly volumes published in Germany.

Vera Vance, born and educated in Sweden, published an essay on the Guermantes as Birds in Proust's *A la recherche du temps perdu* (*French Review*) and a collection of short storeis by H. C. Branner in English translation (*Two Minutes of Silence*). Her own poems have appeared in *Granite, Paintbrush, Humanist*, the women's anthology *Tilt*, and various small magazines.

FREDERIC WILL is a professor of comparative literature at the University of Massachusetts, Amherst, and has taught at Dartmouth

College, Pennsylvania State University, the University of Texas, and the University of Iowa. He received the B.A. degree from Indiana University in 1949 and the Ph.D. from Yale University in 1954. He directed the Translation Workshop at the University of Iowa from 1964 to 1971 and regularly teaches a translation course at Massachusetts.

Will's poetry includes *Mosaic* (1959), *A Wedge of Words* (1962), *Planets* (1966), *Brandy in the Snow* (1972), *Guatemala* (1973), *Botulism* (1975), and *Epics of America* (1977). Among his translations are Kostes Palamas's *The Twelve Words of the Gypsy* (1964) and *The King's Flute* (1967); and Theodor W. Adorno's *The Jargon of Authenticity* (with Knut Tarnowski, 1973). His translations have appeared in *Chicago Review, Texas Quarterly*, and *New Hungarian Quarterly*. He translates from French, German, Spanish, modern Greek, Polish, Hungarian, Norwegian, Swedish, Icelandic, Manx, and several American Indian languages. Will is founder and editor of the translation magazine *Micromegas*.

Dates of First Book Publication

Dates of First Book Publication

Åkesson

Fatum   1966
To Be an Infant   1965
What Does Your Color Red Look Like?   1962

Berggren

Lynäs, a Quartet   1976
A Summer Evening at Slite   1976
Song of Time, at the Sea   1976

Forssell

Mariage avec Dieu   1964
I Sleep in You   1960
Dedication   1960
Van Gogh's Ear   1968
The Chameleon   1968
"Are you looking for a seeing-eye dog"   1971
"Who does not remember Noah . . ."   1972
Tanguy   1975
Wild Rabbits   1975

Friberg

The Journey through Andromeda   1976

Gustafsson

The Wright Brothers Arrive at Kitty Hawk   1968
The Balloon Travelers   1962
"The Perfectionists'" Colony in Oneida, N.Y.   1968
The Machines   1966
Brief Treatise on Seeing and Being Seen   1972
Lines for the Prince of Venosa   1972
Sestina on a Successful Volley   1977

267

Harding   Owl   1975
                     Lasse-Maja in Carlsten Prison   1975
                     The Black Death   1975

Key-Åberg   "Dear life please hurry"   1957
                     "There's a smell of varnish . . ."   1957
                     "The long leagues to the church"   1954
                     "He staggers toward the woodshed"   1954
                     "Round as a seal cub"   1954
                     "What a multitude of gleaming heads"   1963
                     "Have you seen them, . . ."   1972
                     "Sure, I see you, old man"   1972
                     "Look, what huge . . ."   1972

Lundkvist   "Rowanberry time . . ."   1961
                     "It was so dark . . ."   1964
                     "Man across the moor . . ."   1964
                     "Blue mountains . . ."   1964
                     "Pasture burnt, . . ."   1953
                     "Lightning in the ground: . . ."   1953
                     "Something fell down . . ."   1964
                     "Once much ice was here . . ."   1964
                     Event   1969
                     Dryad   1974
                     The Fanatic   1974

Norén   Written around a Joyful Self-Portrait   1972
                     German Song   1973
                     Everything Is Sorted Out   1974
                     "Today everything"   1973
                     "Grasshoppers with gray wings"   1974
                     Thirty Words about Flanders   1972
                     "Woodcutters in white summer shirts"   1974
                     "In the Imperial War Museum"   1974
                     On Nelly Sachs   1976
                     "Listening to the way . . ."   1976
                     "I talk, these days . . ."   1976
                     "Black car shining . . ."   1976

"While we were still sitting . . ."   1976
"Maybe this road"   1976
"Two magical horses . . ."   1976
"When I travel back . . ."   1976

Palm The Sergeant   1964
"When death frightens, . . ."   1971
114/"Why don't the nights . . ."   1971
120/"Suddenly we have a daughter . . ."   1971

Renberg From Home   1974
Drawing   1974
The Farewell Letter   1974
At an Outdoor Café   1974
Morning Conversation   1974
Prayer to My Joy   1974
Weekend (unpublished)
Movies (unpublished)
Things You Can't Talk About . . . (unpublished)
Isaac Newton's Second Wakening (unpublished)
Declaration   1974

Sjöstrand All poems from 1967

Sonnevi Zero   1967
"You are a murderer"   1967
Through the Open Door   1970
The Double Movement   1970
A Ball   1970
On the War in Vietnam   1965
Will Come in Here and Get Your Cap On!   1967
"You shouted to me . . ."   1970
The Island of Koster, 1973   1975

Tranströmer Solitary Swedish Houses   1958
Allegro   1962
After Attack   1958
Morning Birds   1966
Farther In   1973

The Outpost   1973
Baltics   1974
Citoyens   1978
Funchal   1978
The Crosswalk   1978
From the Winter, 1947   1978

6

5